EDUCATING TRAU

EDUCATING TRAUMATIZED CHILDREN

Waldorf Education in Crisis Intervention

BERND RUF

Translation by Margot M. Saar

LINDISFARNE BOOKS | 2013

2013
LINDISFARNE BOOKS
An imprint of SteinerBooks / Anthroposophic Press, Inc.
610 Main Street, Great Barrington, MA 01230
www.steinerbooks.org

Copyright © 2013 by Bernd Ruf. All rights reserved. No part of this book may be reproduced, stored in a retrieval system, or transmitted in any form or by any means, electronic, mechanical, photocopying, recording, or otherwise, without the written permission of Lindisfarne Books. *Educating Traumatized Children* is a translation by Margot M. Saar from German of the book *Trümmer und Traumata: Anthroposophische Grundlagen notfallpädagogischer Einsätze* (Verlag des Ita Wegman Instituts, 2012)

Front cover image: © Eimantas Buzas (shutterstock.com)
Design: William Jens Jensen

Publication of this work was made possible by a grant from the Waldorf Curriculum Fund.

LIBRARY OF CONGRESS CONTROL NUMBER: 2013946282

ISBN: 978-1-58420-155-7 (paperback)
ISBN: 978-1-58420-156-4 (ebook)

Contents

	Preface by Peter Selg	vii
1.	Earthquake, Tsunami, Nuclear Disaster: *Trying to Cope—Somehow*	1
2.	Psychological Trauma: *When Nothing Is as It Used to Be*	7
3.	Emergency Education: *Bringing Healing to Injured Souls*	64
4.	Healing the Frozenness of Trauma: *First Aid for the Souls of Japan's Traumatized Children*	85
5.	Emergency Education as Threshold Education: *An Anthroposophically Extended Understanding of Disaster and Trauma*	129
6.	Competence in Stress Management	173
7.	Crises Can Be Opportunities	184
	Bibliography	189
	About the Author	208

Preface

> How do we proceed with such important matters so that, by cultivating the right attitude and taking the right actions, we might even prevent certain developments? Because that also is part of our task since Anthroposophy would be meaningless if we only practiced it privately for ourselves. —Ita Wegman, 1933

ITA WEGMAN (1876–1943) WAS A PHYSICIAN, head of her own hospital and a promoter of curative education homes and day centers. She was not referring to emergency education when she wrote the above words to Daniel Nicol Dunlop. She was talking about opposing the Nazis and about protecting Jewish friends and children with special needs whose lives were greatly endangered. But her words are nevertheless well suited as an introduction to this book.

The author, Bernd Ruf, cofounder of the Parzival School for multiply challenged children in Karlsruhe, Germany, has initiated and been actively involved in emergency education missions for many years, heading interventions in crisis and disaster areas all over the world. He not only describes the effective educational methods he and his team are applying with traumatized children, but explains the foundations underlying these methods. He is the first person to provide an in-depth account of the anthroposophic view of crisis and trauma in relation to the specialist literature available today in the fields of physiology and psychology. Based on anthroposophic human studies, Bernd Ruf has developed a method that proves the efficacy and practicability of Rudolf Steiner's Waldorf education in caring for massively traumatized children. From his extensive considerations he concludes that natural and accidental disasters are part of our times and of the "human condition." For Bernd Ruf, emergency education is "threshold education." It is brought to bear at the boundaries of life and death where we are, individually and as a society, faced with situations that lead to dissociation but also provide the opportunity for support, therapy, and inner growth. "Where there is danger, there are sustaining powers" (Friedrich Hölderlin).

Bernd Ruf's monograph is a textbook of anthroposophic emergency education that brings readers face to face with the destiny of children and parents. In calling attention to these destinies the book ensures that these victims will not be forgotten. Ruf's deep concern for the individuals he describes renders his account profoundly ethical. The reports we read from Japan and other countries are deeply shocking, and they illustrate, in a more poignant and haunting way than the media does, what is going on day in, day out in disaster and crisis areas of the world. But the reports also speak of interventions that help victims move on. Ruf's book is a scientific textbook as well as an appeal for action. Even esoteric aspects are looked at in relation to their practical significance for everyday life, as a basis for taking action out of insight.

Bernd Ruf's book was written in the year of Rudolf Steiner's 150th birthday. It was never Rudolf Steiner's intention to found elite schools. His aim was to introduce a new art of education for *all* children and adolescents, but mostly for children who have to struggle with obstacles and difficult life situations. A hundred years after Rudolf Steiner's first lectures on an education enhanced by spiritual science (1906) the Friends of Waldorf Education introduced emergency education in Lebanon (2006). Since then there have been many assignments and new missions at a time when one disaster seems to follow another, threatening and questioning the foundations of our earthly biographies. Bernd Ruf's book evokes many existential questions, explicitly as well as by implication. But while it raises more questions than it provides answers, the book invokes new perspectives and hopes for the future. Emergency education relies on timeliness—on intervention at an early stage, at a time when silence, despondency, despair, and regression begin to set in. Emergency education is not trauma therapy. It is pedagogical prevention of trauma in the early stages of a crisis and as such it attempts to "prevent certain developments by cultivating the right attitude and taking the right actions." "Our actions invite the benignity of the gods" (Ita Wegman).

Professor Peter Selg, MD
Ita Wegman Institute
for Basic Research into Anthroposophy
Arlesheim, February 2012

I

Earthquake, Tsunami, Nuclear Disaster

Trying to Cope—Somehow

Japan's Black Day

> "I had just picked up my five-year-old daughter from kindergarten and we were on our way home when the earth started trembling," Sugawara[1] (43) reports. "The tremor was severe and lasted for about three minutes, so I knew there was the danger of a tsunami. I fled, along with neighbors and thousands of other people from Onagawa, to our local hospital that stands on a hill above the town. I saw that people had climbed onto the roof of the bank, a high building below the hospital—in vain; the entire building was flooded. Later, we saw cars stranded on the roofs of other high buildings. Suddenly, masses of people pushed their way up to the higher floors of the hospital. My daughter and I reached the second floor. What happened next I cannot believe to this day. The tsunami came right up to the hospital that stands thirty meters above the town. Everyone on the ground floor—patients and rescue-seekers—was drowned. I watched from the window as my hometown of Onagawa was washed away. My daughter and I now live in a three-square-meter cardboard box in the gym hall which we share with thousands of neighbors. We lost everything except our lives."

March 11, 2011, was Japan's black day.[2] At 2:45 p.m. local time, northern Japan was shaken by the most ferocious earthquake in the country's history. The epicenter of the quake was off the coast of

---

1. Names were changed by the author for privacy reasons.
2. Erdbeben und Tsunami: Japans schwarzer Tag. http://www.spiegel.de /panorama/0,518,druck-750449html; March 11, 2001, 8:54 p.m.

A landscape of ruins in the crisis zone

Fukushima, at a depth of about 30 kilometers. Around 40 minutes later a gigantic brownish-grey wave washed over the northeastern coast of Japan with unimaginable speed. The mass of water left behind destruction of apocalyptic dimensions. The tsunami tore off coast fortifications and washed over a 470-square-kilometer area, pushing 40 kilometers inland up the riverbeds. Whole cities and towns were carried away and entirely destroyed by the floods. A deadly deluge of houses, ships, cars, railway carriages, containers and other debris buried the coastal region along a stretch of 350 kilometers. The prefectures of Miyagi, Iwate and Fukushima were among the worst affected.[3] Around seven million homes were left without electricity and about a million homes had no drinking water. Two hundred thousand houses

---

3. "Tsunami-Katastrophe in Japan: Flutwelle löscht Küstenstadt aus"; http://www.spiegel.de/panorama/0,1518,druck-750564.00html; March 12, 2011, 4:15 p.m.

were left uninhabitable. The government sent a hundred thousand soldiers to the disaster area for rescue work.[4]

As a result of the earthquake and the tsunami, the nuclear power plant in Fukushima was severely damaged,[5] undergoing a reactor melt-down and several explosions and releasing radioactive material in the process. On March 29, 2011, radiation levels measured at sea near the coast of Fukushima were 3,355 times the legal limit.[6] An area of 30 kilometers around the nuclear plant was closed off and approximately 80,000 people were evacuated. It is only thanks to favorable meteorological conditions that Japan was not more severely contaminated. The wind blew the radioactive material that had leaked out of the plant out to the open sea where the contaminated cooling water from the reactors was also dumped. Many experts worldwide see the nuclear accident in Fukushima, 66 years after the atomic bombs were dropped on the Japanese cities of Hiroshima and Nagasaki, as the biggest nuclear disaster since the 1979 partial meltdown at Three Mile Island nuclear power station in Pennsylvania and the 1986 explosion at reactor block 4 in Chernobyl.

Sendai, a city in the north of Japan with a population of one million, was hit hardest. Sendai is situated approximately 130 kilometers south of the epicenter of the earthquake and around 80 kilometers from Fukushima. Whole districts were washed away by the floods, trains were carried away, oceangoing yachts were flushed onto the roofs of high buildings. At the coast, hundreds of dead bodies floated in the sea or were washed ashore.[7]

---

4. Eine Million Haushalte ohne Trinkwasser. http://www.spiegel.de/panorama/0,1518,druck-750629.00html; March 13, 2011, 9:30 a.m.

5. "Explosion im Kernkraftwerk: Japan erlebt eine nukleare Katastrophe"; http://www.spiegel.de/wissenschaft/technik/0,1518,druck-750479.00html; March 12, 2011, 9:03 a.m.

6. "AKW-Havarie: Strahlung im Meer vor Fukushima steigt auf Rekordwert"; http://www.spiegel.de/panorama/0,1518,druck-753933.00html; March 30, 2011, 7:37 a.m.

7. See footnote 3, page 2.

The authorities estimate that around 25,000 people were killed or lost, but the actual number of victims is likely much higher because in many cases no one was left who could report those missing. Months after the disaster, 190,000 people still live in 1,350 emergency shelters. Severe aftershocks keep the survivors in a state of constant fear and terror, evoking horrendous memories of the disaster.[8]

After the material damage caused by the earthquake and the tsunami, people's souls were overwhelmed by an inner tsunami that was no less severe. Many are injured and traumatized. The threat of mental scars is omnipresent. "My life has become ash-grey. I can hardly remember what happened. There is still a huge gap in my memory. But when I remember something, my whole body begins to shake!" says Toshi (29), a teacher from Sendai, and his colleague Hiroki (32) adds, "We try to cope—somehow!"

Many of the evacuated children are frightened and traumatized. "They are surrounded by scenes of devastation. All they see are destroyed houses and upside-down cars. These are shocking pictures for them," says Ian Woolverton of the aid organization Save the Children. "Once the children can laugh again it will do the adults good. It helps everybody!"[9]

From April 27 to May 10, 2011, a ten-person emergency education team[10] was sent to Sendai by the aid organization Friends of Waldorf Education. They were joined by anthroposophic physicians, therapists,

---

8. "Japanisches Katastrophengebiet von neuem Beben erschüttert"; http://stern.de/news2/aktuell/japanisches-katastrophengebiet-von-neuem-beben-erschüttert...html; May 15, 2011.

9. "Notunterkünfte im Katastrophengebiet: 700 Menschen in einem Raum"; http://www.spiegel.de/panorama/gesellschaft/0,1518,druck-751897.00html; March 19, 2011, 11"32 a.m.

10. The emergency education team included: Susan Gay (art therapist), Monika Görzel-Straube (teacher), Bärbel Irion, MD (psychiatrist and psychotherapist); Gritt Malsch (teacher), Jörg Merzenich special needs teacher), Akiko Matsunga (eurythmist), Sibylle Naito (teacher), Markus Seitz (logistics), Mechthild Pellmann (art therapist), Bernd Ruf (Special needs teacher and team leader).

teachers, and educators from all over Japan to work with traumatized children, teachers, and parents on processing their horrific experiences so they would not develop posttraumatic stress disorders and psychopathologies in the aftermath of the disaster.

Will These Wounds Ever Heal?

Every hour, somewhere in the world, children are experiencing the inconceivable as they fall victim to war or displacement. Children suffer maltreatment, abuse, and neglect; they witness and experience natural and human-caused disasters. When the inconceivable happens their lives change forever. The younger children are when they suffer extreme stress and the closer they are to the perpetrator, the more severe and lasting are the consequences of their trauma (Krüger, 2007b, 47).

How can we, through education, help children and adolescents in war and crisis areas to overcome severe trauma? How can parents, educators, and teachers help children and adolescents in distressing life situations? How can Waldorf education become emergency education?

The following chapters describe examples of emergency education for children and adolescents who have lived through inconceivable ordeals. As a response to the extreme stress they were exposed to, victims display a multitude of symptoms. They are struggling to come to terms with what they suffered. If they cannot resolve their trauma they may develop posttraumatic stress disorder and even experience a disruption of their biography.

Since 2006, the aid organization Friends of Waldorf Education has been carrying out interventions in disaster areas evolved from Waldorf education (Kiersch, 1997; Leber, 1992; Loebell, 2011). This emergency education has helped many children in all parts of the world cope with the aftermath of wars and natural disasters.

Victims of disasters try to cope—somehow. Following the introduction in chapter 1, chapter 2 of this book explains the concept of trauma. For someone who has experienced trauma, nothing will ever be as it used to be. What is trauma? What kinds of trauma are there? What makes difficult experiences traumatic? What neurobiological changes are involved? What happens after the trauma? This book provides an outline of the current state of research into child trauma.

Emergency education tries to heal wounded souls. Chapter 3 describes the origin and history of emergency education and the Waldorf approach to supporting traumatized children. *Emergency education is First Aid for the child soul.* Chapter 4 presents the guidelines of emergency education and describes assignments carried out by the aid organization Friends of Waldorf Education in war or disaster areas, particularly after the triple disaster in Northern Japan.

Emergency Education happens in places of outer and inner chaos. It is education at the threshold. Chapter 5 explains anthropological-anthroposophic aspects that can contribute to a wider understanding of trauma and disaster.

Part 6 describes aspects of real posttraumatic growth and the positive biographical effects trauma can have once it has been resolved. Every crisis is also an opportunity. Trauma education seizes this opportunity.

2

Psychological Trauma

When Nothing Is as It Used to Be

Trauma Can Change Lives Forever

Consider the massacre on the Norwegian island of Utoya or the devastation caused by a tsunami in Northern Sumatra; think of the floods that buried New Orleans after Hurricane Katrina or the mass panic at the Love Parade in Duisburg, Germany. And consider the extremist suicide attack in Mumbai, the severe earthquake in the Chinese province of Sichuan, the famine in the Horn of Africa or the nuclear contamination in Fukushima in Northern Japan. When the unconceivable happens nothing will be as before. When horrific disasters such as these that may strike anywhere in the world occur, brutal violence and existential fears "hit people's lives like a hammer or corrode them like an acid" (Donowitz and Lache, 2011, 74). Trauma changes the lives of victims forever. It changes the way they think, feel, and act; it changes their values and causes them to think differently of themselves and of the world.

Teddy was nine months old when he was rushed to hospital with a severe allergic reaction. He was strapped to an examination table; his whole body was prodded by a team of dermatologists. The child, exposed to glaring lights and unable to move, screamed in terror throughout the whole procedure. After the examination, he was placed in isolation for a week. His mother was not allowed to visit him. When Teddy was discharged he did not recognize his mother. "She claims that the boy never connected again with her or any other family member. He did not bond with other children, grew increasingly isolated and began living in a world of his own" (Levine and Kline, 2008, 103). One can assume that the trauma experienced in hospital profoundly affected later developments in the personality of Theodore Kaczynski. Between 1978 and 1995 he dispatched letter bombs to technology firms, university professors and airlines, killing three and injuring 23. Theodore Kaczynski is the "Unabomber." Psychologists say his actions are a revenge campaign on "the same dehumanizing forces that overcame and broke him as an infant" (ibid., 103).

Children are not born as "blank slates." The spiritual dimension, which we experience as the child's individuality and which the child will later refer to as "I," exists before the physical birth and connects with the physical body in the process of incarnation (Selg, 2010). When children are born they bring with them their own individual life goals. Right from the start, they are looking for their identity and for ways of realizing their biographies. Children shape their own lives. "The birth of a child is not a coincidence. The child has sought out this life and is always looking for ways of shaping the life he or she has sought.... The child's foremost goal is to grow up and live his or her biography in a place that is secure—physically, emotionally and socially" (van der Stel, 2011, 173).

Dannion Brinkley was sent on a secret US Army mission during the Vietnam War. He was a member of the Secret Service's killer commando force responsible for liquidating politically and militarily undesirable persons in Southeast Asia and Central America. He killed dozens of people. He says that, as a child, he was only interested in technical things and extremely aggressive: "I had been uncontrollable and proud of it" (Brinkley and Perry, 1994, 11). He stole, bullied and tormented. He says he must have had six thousand fights between class 5 and class 12: "My father didn't mean any harm.... He showed me how to make a blackjack out of a pair of my mother's nylon stockings by pouring sand into them and tying the ends" (Ibid., 12). When

Dannion joined the army he received special training to channel his aggression.

Dannion Brinkley does not reveal any more details of his childhood, but it can be assumed that he was multiply traumatized. Victims become perpetrators, but perpetrators continue to be traumatized by their own actions: "Now they call students like that 'hyperactive' and do something about it. Back then we were just called 'bad kids' and were thought to be lost causes" (ibid., 11f.).

In 1975, Dannion Brinkley was struck by lightning while speaking on the phone. Twenty minutes later he was resuscitated. In his book *Saved by the Light* (1994) he described his experiences at the threshold of death: he saw the consequences of his actions from the victim's point of view, experienced how his murders impacted the lives of relatives, and realized the extent to which he had deviated from his original life intentions: "As my body lay dead on that stretcher, I was reliving every moment of my life.... Not only could I feel the way both I and the other person had felt when an incident took place, I could also feel the feelings of the next person they reacted to" (Ibid., 14). He then decided to resume his life. Just before the successful resuscitation, he had a vision of his future life. His prenatal decisions, his life motifs, and impulses appeared to him in images. After his reanimation he wrote down 117 of those images. Eighteen years later, when he wrote his book, 95 of them had become reality. Since his return to life, Dannion Brinkley has been working for the American hospice movement.

Many near-death experiences feature prophetic visions or images of a future life. The findings of near-death research are confirmed by Rudolf Steiner's spiritual science. Before birth "we have a moment of vision, similar to the moment after death when we look back over our life. But it is an anticipation of the future.... Very young children sometimes speak of such experiences, before they take on the materialist views of their surroundings. We anticipate our future existence. These are two essential moments because they show us what we bring to our new incarnation. When we die, this knowledge is a memory. When we reincarnate it is a vision of the future" (Steiner, 1976, CW 93a, 159).

Once we are born, our prenatal images that contain motifs of our future life, sink down in the subconscious. When we reach puberty, at around the age of seventeen, our prenatal decisions can light up as images in our soul. If they are not suppressed due to cultural influences or traumatic events, they can rise to consciousness as ideals. Today's materialist culture often hinders these motifs from rising up into the young person's consciousness. But they continue to stir deep down, subconsciously, and transform into counter-images. "If we have this experience…we know what the human soul is capable of and we know one thing in particular—once turned into their opposites, the noblest spiritual aims can be transformed into the most horrible deeds in the physical world. We will know that, in the depths of the soul, the noblest intentions of sacrifice can turn into the desire to kill" (Steiner, 1976, CW 145, 144). As a result of this kind of transformation we see apathy, depression, aggression, brutality, delinquency, and even suicidal tendencies.

Two streams come together when a child is born; our spirit-soul arrives from its prenatal existence and unites with the physical foundations we inherit from our parents. If the situation we are born into does not prove conducive to our individual life aims, if subtle abnormalities hinder or prevent our individuality from realizing our life intentions, the spirit-soul will feel imprisoned in the body and it will try to destroy this prison by breaking out of it.

Rudolf Steiner spoke of the possible consequences of such a development in strong terms. "The most horrid, evil passions come to light; horrific errors. Where do they come from? They are not all due to an evil disposition. Partly they are caused by the individuality's inability to find the right organs for realizing its good intentions in this incarnation. It might feel relief when these intentions tear apart the surrounding shell so it can create better foundations for a future incarnation" (Steiner, 1984, CW 118, 59). Today's psychology considers manslaughter as a possible result of repressed suicide and violent behavior as repressed self-aggression.

Many people today suffer from latent trauma and wounds to their soul that keep them from finding meaning in their life without necessarily committing murder or suicide. "It does not always manifest in such radical ways but comes to expression in the feelings—which are so prevalent today—of dissatisfaction, hopelessness, not knowing what to do with oneself, especially between the ages of 14 or 15 and 21. It lingers and cannot be remedied in this life. An inner mood of hopelessness prevails, a lack of direction, a sense of pessimism and dissatisfaction" (Ibid., 60).

Trauma can disrupt the incarnating process and conceal the prenatal motifs, leading to a profound personal crisis. Trauma victims suffer "from a sense of meaninglessness and emptiness, an existential vacuum" (Frankl, 2008, 184). The loss of meaning often triggers existential fear. Afflicted persons are not just afraid because of what they did but also because of what they omitted to do. The lack of meaning in their lives will ultimately elicit compensatory behavior: "Overcome by senselessness and exposed to an all-pervading inner emptiness, they will seek adventures aimlessly in order to fill the inner emptiness with non-sense, with absurdity.... This lack of meaning is the cause also of the increasing global incidence of aggression, delinquency, drug addiction and suicide" (Ibid., 185, trans. revised). Such untapped resources and impulses that are not brought to realization can become destructive. Good can turn into evil.

Trauma is like a tremor in the soul. It shakes up the inner landscape and can bring whole regions of the soul to collapse. Trauma can block off a child's path through life, causing it to "end in meaninglessness" (ibid., 45).

Grief and Trauma Are Not the Same

Mieko (9) is in class four at the Fujino Waldorf School. On 12 March, after the explosion of reactor I at Fukushima Daiichi, she flees with her parents and her sister Kurumi Mioko (6). On the evening of 2 May, Kurumi Mioko is hit by a car in Oita, a refugee camp in the south. She dies instantly. The family receives counseling from a Christian Community priest. While the parents cannot come to terms with the death of their child and are close to a breakdown, Mieko displays no conspicuous or worrying behaviors. She comforts her mother and speaks to her grandparents on the phone about her sister's death. "She might be a bit shyer or clingier since the accident. Sometimes she is sad, sometimes angry" says her father, Katsonube (35). Mieko does not show any particular signs of trauma at that point. She is grieving.

Mourning is part of life. It is our response to feelings of loss—death, divorce, the leaving of important attachment figures, maltreatment, abuse, or neglect, fires, earthquakes, floods or other natural disasters. "The sense of the world as a safe place is gone" (Levine and Kline, 2008, 159). But while it is possible to have grief without trauma, it is "not possible to have trauma without grief" (ibid., 159).

It makes a difference to our ability to cope with a loss whether it was expected, we were able to say goodbye, or the loss was sudden and unexpected. The processes of grieving and trauma are very similar, while the processes of resolving them don't have to be.

Elisabeth Kübler-Ross (1983) described grieving as a five-stage process; our first reaction to an experience of loss is denial. We **"don't want to know,"** withdraw, and become isolated. We are numb with shock. When children become frozen in response to loss, they need to receive emotional first aid to release the frozen "survival energy" (Levine and Kline, 2008, 40). During the second stage of the grieving process we experience **anger, wrath, and sadness** about the loss. Often we feel empty, irritable, disappointed, and worried. Anger is an important and normal emotion in this situation. Children who can express their feelings are beginning to leave the state of frozenness and powerlessness behind. Tears can be liberating! Kübler-Ross referred to the third stage of the grieving process as **bargaining.** Strong feelings of guilt can arise at this stage. The child or adolescent regrets what they did or did not do. When children or adolescents are burdened by their actions or omissions they need help to express these feelings so they can find closure or let go. They must be encouraged and supported by the adults who they feel close to. Children should never be burdened with the pain of their parents. After a fourth stage of **depression** the grieving process ends with its final stage, **acceptance**.

Grieving children and adolescents need psychological support. They need adult help with processing their painful emotions. Each of the stages of grieving described can be supported with special rituals that alleviate the grieving process and help to bring it to a successful conclusion (Glöckler and Heine, 2003; Hermann, 2005; Wais and Schellenberg, 1998; German Ministry of Culture, Youth and Sports, Baden Wurttemberg, 2004).

The trauma process usually proceeds in four phases (Cullberg, 1978). The initial phase of **shock** (numbness, chaotic actions) is followed by the **reaction phase** (confronting reality, attempting integration) and that is followed by the **adjustment phase** (process of understanding and clarification, detachment from the trauma). A successful trauma resolution process ends with a phase of **reorientation** (gaining a new sense of self-worth, building up new relationships).

Despite some essential similarities between trauma and grief, there are obvious differences that one needs to be aware of. As part of a sociological study, William Steele and Melvyn Raider (2001, 155) listed the following differences between trauma and grief responses. While the grieving process involves feelings of sadness that have no effect on the griever's self-image or self-confidence, trauma evokes a sense of horror and overwhelming powerlessness and leads to a loss of any sense of safety, a distorted self-image and the loss of self-reliance. Grief results in despondence while trauma leads to silent suffering. Talking about their pain can bring relief to mourners, while the means of verbal expression tend to be blocked in trauma sufferers. Mourners do not tend to the violent acting-out of their loss, while the anger of trauma victims often finds expression in (self-) aggression. Grieving children often dream of the deceased person, while traumatized children have nightmares in which they appear themselves as possible victims. Finally, grief heals with time while traumatic experiences, if not resolved, tend to manifest in increasing and aggravated symptoms.

Grieving children must not be left to themselves. Mieko needed support. Stories and fairy tales nurture the soul, especially in difficult times. It is important for a child's grieving process that feelings and thoughts are allowed and can be expressed. "Mourning, if repressed, will be a hindrance in life" (Hermann, 2005, 4). Feelings and thoughts can be creatively expressed through painting and drawing. Fostering spiritual or religious feelings can help children process experiences of loss, independently of any particular denomination. Prayers can instill life forces, as can age-appropriate conversations with children about existential questions or looking at pictures of angels. "I knew that being pious meant health and serenity" (Hesse, quoted in ibid., 6). Nature observation can also restore new trust in the wisdom and order of life; the metamorphosis from larva to butterfly, for instance, can be a helpful image.

Rituals can help sufferers cope with the inconceivable. You can plant a little tree for the dead person, celebrate the day of death as a heavenly birthday, or include the person who has passed away into the festivals of the year.

It is necessary to help children and young people to separate trauma and grief. The work of mourning can only begin once the "shock energy" has been dissipated. It needs trauma resolution to set the child or adolescent free from a traumatic fixation with the past and allow the healing process of mourning to begin. "When trauma is resolved children can get on with the business of both grieving and living. When it is not they may easily get stuck in a fantasy of how it was then—before the 'terrible thing' happened—rather than be in the reality of now. The result is a failure to develop emotionally. There remains a disruption of a child's life, as if frozen in time" (Levine and Kline, 2008, 162).

> Mieko goes to the Waldorf school in Fujino. Her sister Kurumi Mioko, who died, used to go to the Waldorf Kindergarten in Kito. The other children in the kindergarten respond to the accident with grief, questions, and anxiety. They need help with coming to terms with the loss.

When a child dies not only the family needs support but the kindergarten group or school class also needs to be included in the mourning process. It is not a matter of "providing ready-made answers. It is a matter of not running away because one feels helpless but having the courage to provide closeness, presence, humanity even if there is nothing that can be healed on the outside" (Hermann, 2005, 6).

It is important to give a special place to the mourning. This can be a central space in the school or kindergarten such as a classroom or a meeting room. "Often, a table is set up with a picture of the deceased person; candles and flower decorations, a bible, a book for people to write down their thoughts and feelings" (Ministry of Culture, Youth and Sports in Baden Wurttemberg, Germany, 2004, 13). When a period of time has passed, a tree can be planted for the deceased child in the school grounds that the classmates look after. The grave is also such a place of mourning.

Shared mourning rituals are as important as mourning places; moments of silence, handmade gifts for decorating the grave or memorial site, letters or drawings for the deceased or a chair circle with a cloth in the middle on which a candle is placed for the deceased child: "When so many children died in the great earthquake in Kobe in 1995, the chairs of those children remained empty for the rest of the school year. A photo of each child and flowers were placed on their desks. At the end of the school year, when prizes were given out as is the custom there, the prizes for the deceased children did not go to others but were handed over to their fathers or mothers. This allows not only the relatives but all pupils to have the experience; Kim is dead but he has a place in our lives, and we celebrate what he achieved with us in school" (Hermann, 2005, 8f.).

Mieko's mother Yumi (33) lived in Kobe twelve years ago when she and her family became victims of an earthquake. They were rescued, but their home was destroyed in the disaster.

Trauma Disrupts a Person's Inner Organization

Trauma injures, hinders, and destroys. It ruins relationships, disrupts people's connection with their environment, and causes them to feel disconnected from their body.

Trauma Damages Our Bio-Psychosocial-Spiritual Wholeness

In the early twentieth century Rudolf Steiner presented a "holistic image of the human being as a bio-psychosocial-spiritual entity" (Niemeijer, 2011a, 96). Waldorf education is based on this image of clearly distinguishable levels of the organization of the human being (Steiner, 1987, CW 34, 312ff.; Selg 2006, 97ff.). If someone is traumatized, these levels can no longer function or mutually interact in a healthy way:

- The **physical body** is part of the earthly-material substance world and, like all things of the material world, it is subject to the laws of gravity. The physical body is made up of the substances of the physical world that create their own boundaries.

    Traumatized children lose or break off the connection with their physical body or parts of it. As a consequence they lose their spatial orientation. Their basic senses (sense of touch, sense of life, sense of movement, sense of balance) stop developing and remain immature. When their basic senses become dysfunctional children develop severe emotional and behavioral problems. Traumatized children often also lose contact

with the world around them. They tend to misplace things and neglect their clothes or other personal possessions.
- Up until the moment when we die our physical body is continuously permeated and enlivened by the life body (ether body). As soon as this life principle leaves the physical body the latter begins to decay. The life body is apparent in phenomena such as growth, nurture, healing, reproduction, circulation, regeneration, etc. All functions of the life body have a temporal dimension. "The ether body manifests in the interaction and synchronization of hundreds of rhythms. Each of these rhythms triggers a particular process and all of them together maintain the organism" (Lievegoed, 2002, 213). Life is rhythm!

The life body is in charge of transforming and absorbing the substances we take in from the outside world and for adapting them to the special conditions that prevail in our physical body. It is also the carrier of our memory that explains why our past life appears to us in a panoramic review in the moment of death, when the life body leaves the physical body.

We differentiate four kinds of ether in relation to this life body (Steiner, 1978, CW 212, Lecture of 28 May 1922; Lievegoed, 2002, 163f.):

- The **life ether** (form or crystal ether) tends toward rigidity. Its rhythms give matter a geometrical-crystalline form. The life ether has a particular relationship with the human body.
- The rhythms of the **chemical ether** (sound ether) bring order to matter when in the liquid state. The chemical ether is responsible for the many chemical processes in our metabolism. Rhythmic irregularities in the chemical ether will manifest instantly in chemical reactions in the fluid organism, with substances being produced that are not normally present there.

- The rhythms of the **light ether** (consciousness ether) manifest primarily in the neurosensory system, which constitutes the physical foundation of consciousness. The rhythms of the light ether appear in the electrical nerve impulses traceable through electroencephalography (EEG). The light ether is related to the soul or astral body.
- In the circulating blood the **warmth ether** permeates the entire organism and the other ethers. The warmth ether has a particular relationship with our self, or "I" (our spiritual dimension), for it is through the blood that our I takes hold of the rest of our organization.

Disruptions of the various rhythms of the life body manifest first and foremost as disturbances in our organic functions. These disturbances are relatively easy to treat in the initial stages but can cause irreversible organ deformations if their causes are not removed. Our soul or astral body, as the carrier of mental images, emotions and drives, has an influence on the rhythms of the life body and can therefore cause blockages or damage to the life and physical bodies.

Traumatized children become detached from their life body. As a result of this detachment, the central nervous system cannot grow and mature as it should, which leads to developmental delay. As symptoms one observes phenomena such as regression to baby language, thumb sucking, or bed-wetting. Because these children's immune systems are weakened they become more susceptible to allergies and infections and their wounds don't heal well. The life rhythms of traumatized children are often disrupted and this manifests in sleep and eating disorders. Traumatized children tend to have a disturbed relationship with time and a weak sense of rhythm. Because many of their biological rhythms are dysfunctional their whole sense of being is undermined.

Trauma causes psychosomatic symptoms. Traumatized children respond to emotional stress with stomachaches and headaches.

Many children develop memory problems after traumatic experiences and end up having learning difficulties or learning disorders. Traumatized children tend to sap their own (etheric) life forces because of their self-aggressive and self-harming behaviors.

- The **soul body (astral body)**, the third level of our organization according to the anthroposophic human studies, is the seat of feelings and emotions such as sympathy and antipathy, desires and passions, aggression, etc. as well as the carrier of the soul forces of thinking, feeling, and will.

Movement, experience, and conscious awareness are features of the soul body, which also manifest physically;

Movement appears physically as muscle tension and psychologically as drives and impulses. Experience is reflected physically in respiration and heartbeat and psychologically as feelings and dreams.

Conscious awareness manifests physically as pain and at the soul level as perception and thought processes (Niemeijer, 2011a, 99f.).

Our soul life includes soul qualities that affect the rhythms of the life body and therefore the physical body, as well: "Emotions, mental images or desires accelerate or decelerate certain rhythms. More intense soul movements can bring disorder to these rhythms or even destroy them" (Lievegoed, 2002, 215).

Psychological influences of such a destructive nature can cause noticeable anatomical malformations that are very difficult to treat once they have become chronic.

The human psychosocial organization encompasses seven "character structures" (ibid., 216) or basic inner attitudes. They are like particular colorations of the psyche. The Dutch psychiatrist and former head of the Dutch Pedagogical Institute (NPI), Bernard Lievegoed, (1979, 116ff.) identified the following "character structures," one of which tends to dominate—the investigator, the thinker, the organizer, the innovator, the caregiver and administrator, the creative type, and the compensator (ibid., 118). Each of these basic dispositions can manifest in active-extrovert or passive-introvert ways.

Trauma damages children's soul life by disrupting its development and functions. We see evidence of this in the effect childhood trauma has on soul faculties such as cognition (thinking), emotion (feeling), actions and behaviors (will) the ability to form relationships, the motivation for movement, etc.

Traumatized children break or lose contact with other people. Their attachment behaviors become insecure and disorganized. Most traumatized children are overly alert, emotionally unstable, and hyperactive. They instinctively take recourse in the fight-or-flight response or oppositional behaviors. Whereas seemingly trivial events can evoke impulsive outbreaks in these children, the physical pain of their injuries can go almost unnoticed.

Child trauma leads to the hyper-activation and premature development of the psycho-emotional-social level of the child's organization. As a result the astral body may become injured and damaged.

- The **self, or "I,"** as the fourth level of our organization, regulates the feeling life and keeps desires, drives, and aggressions under control. It is the "I" that sets us apart from animals and their innate and species-specific behavior patterns. The "I" assures that we assimilate experiences. The "I" is the carrier of our individuality or immortal spiritual essence.

At the physical-etheric level we observe the impact of the "I" in a person's uprightness and gait, for instance. At the psychosocial level the "I" regulates thinking, feeling, and will and is evident in faculties such as reflection and self-awareness. The "I" manifests as intelligence in the thinking, it checks the mood swings and emotional outbreaks of our feeling life, and, where the will is concerned, it transforms the physical behavior patterns of animals into goal-oriented actions.

At the spiritual level the "I" manifests in qualities such as morality, conscience, ideals, autonomy, and biographical orientation.

The "I," or self, is not identical with our spiritual individuality. "every individual man carries, within himself, at least in his adaptation and destination, a purely ideal man. The great problem of his existence is to bring all the incessant changes of his outer life into conformity with the unchanging unity of this ideal" (Schiller, letter 4, in *On the Aesthetic Education of Man*). The "I" is more like C. G. Jung's "persona"—that is, a kind of mask that we put on (Kast, 2004, 12f.). Our spiritual essence is concealed behind our everyday self: "What we refer to as 'I' in everyday life is not our true, higher self. It is the mirror image of that higher self" (Lievegoed, 2002, 69) at the physical, etheric and astral levels of our organization.

Severe trauma in early childhood almost always disrupts the development of the child's individuality. The child's "I" is damaged. As a consequence, the child's capacity for empathy, for establishing relationships, for developing self-trust and trust in others is impaired and destroyed. The regulating effect that the "I" should exert on emotions and impulses is blocked or lost. The "I" becomes engulfed in a hyperactive astrality and is literally carried away by emotional outbursts and eruptive impulses.

Furthermore, the "I" loses its ability to process and integrate experiences. Detachment, dissociative behavior, depersonalization, and de-realization, memory problems (amnesia, flashbacks), and the absence of emotional bonding is the results of such disintegration; the "I" loses control.

Trauma Damages the Threefold Human Organization

In his letters *On the Aesthetic Education of Man*, Friedrich Schiller developed an anthropology based on the interaction of three drives: the sensuous drive, the formal drive, and the play drive.

According to Schiller each individual "carries, within himself, at least in his adaptation and destination, a purely ideal man. The great problem of his existence is to bring all the incessant changes of his outer life into conformity with the unchanging unity of this ideal" (Schiller, letter 4). In order for this to be achieved, form manifests in substance (world). Through human's transformation of nature ("cultivation"), human ("person"), and nature achieve perfection.

We are, as human beings, part of the natural world (substance, sensuous world) and subject to its laws. At the level of the **sensuous drive** we are subject to nature's biological and physiological laws, as is apparent in respiration and the ingestion of food. Here, we are not free. The sensuous drive strives to externalize and materialize our inner life. If we give in to the sensuous drive we become egoistic, uncultured, and violent. We will become slaves, driven by our nature, "savages."

By being part of the spiritual world (form) we are subject to its laws of logic and reason. Substance needs to be formed. We are not free in this sphere either. If we fully devote ourselves to the **formal drive** we become slaves of our principles, pedants, fanatics, "barbarians."

The third level lies in the middle and is not determined by the laws of nature or reason. It combines the elements of sensuous and formal drive in an aesthetic state based on the play drive, the free play of forces. "Aesthetic state" means that the demands of reason and nature are brought into harmony by the **play drive**. "We play only when we are truly human, and we are only truly human when we play" (Schiller, letter 15). According to Schiller, it is through aesthetic and artistic activities that we can become balanced, cultured individuals.

Friedrich Schiller's anthropology, as expressed in his letters *On the Aesthetic Education of Man*, can explain the healing influence of aesthetic and artistic pursuits in education and emergency education: "Beauty is the perfect accord of the sensual and the spiritual" (Grillparzer, quoted in Brotbeck, 1959, 18). Trauma can damage or destroy this harmonious accord between the sensual and the spiritual, between spirit-soul and enlivened body.

Rudolf Steiner described his insights into the threefold human organism in his book *Riddles of the Soul*, which was first published in 1917 (Steiner, 1976, CW 21). Every organism has a threefold structure where a form pole and a movement pole are linked by a rhythmic center: "The rhythmic system, which encompasses the functions of blood circulation through the heart and respiration through the lungs, is the foundation for the feeling life. The neurosensory system is the realm of form. It functions primarily from the head and is responsible for perception and thinking. The metabolism/limb system resides in the lower region and constitutes the organic basis for will and actions" (Giesen, 2011, 233). Although the three systems can be clearly distinguished they are not separate from each other. They permeate each other and they permeate the organism as a whole: "These are not parallel, separate activities. They permeate each other and transmute into one another. We have metabolic activity everywhere in the organism; it penetrates the organs of rhythm as well as those of neurosensory activity. But in the rhythm the metabolic activity is not the physical basis of our feeling and in the neurosensory activity it is not the physical basis of our thinking. It remains the foundation of the will, which it carries into the rhythmic and neurosensory processes" (Steiner, 1976, CW 21, 156).

Any trauma-induced damage to the four levels of the human organization (fourfold human organization) described earlier will manifest as developmental disorders, disturbances, or impairments in the systems of the threefold human organization (Niemeijer, 2011b, 104):

- Our **neurosensory organization** has its center in the head and is the basis of perception, thinking and memory. The rhythm of the neurosensory system swings between the poles of remembering and forgetting. The one-sided fixations common after trauma can result in the victim either not being able to forget traumatic images (compulsory memories, flashbacks) or being unable to remember them (amnesia).
- The chest, where heart and lungs reside as the rhythm organs of circulation and respiration respectively, forms the center of our **rhythmic organization** and the basis of our feelings and the capacity for empathy. Here, the pendulum swings between the poles of connecting and detaching. This connecting and letting go applies to the relationship of the spirit-soul and body as well as to the relationship we have to our environment—the relationship between "I and you." Trauma has a long-term effect on these rhythms by holding its victims fixed to one of those poles with the result that they develop breathing, sleeping, or speech disorders. Trauma victims withdraw and become "thick-skinned." Or they grow to be too thin-skinned; they cannot keep themselves separate, but lose themselves in their surroundings.
- The **metabolism/limb organization**, situated in the abdominal area and the limbs, provides the foundation for our metabolic activity and mobility, but also for our will, ability to act, and self-efficacy. The rhythmic pendulum in this area swings between the poles of movement and rest. Trauma-induced fixations at this level result either in frozenness and immobility, or in restlessness and hyperactivity.

Trauma Damages the Connection of "I" and Body

If we are healthy our "I" integrates what we experience into our biography. The "I" takes initiative and regulates or controls emotions, will impulses, and thought processes. When we attain majority, our individuality is sufficiently incarnated so we can lead a responsible life in accordance with our life goals. Before we reach majority we go through a process of incarnating and ripening that proceeds in three seven-year stages. During each of these seven-year periods, the various members of the human organization (levels of existence) develop further and become more individualized. As part of this individualization the "I" manifests in specific ways. This progressing incarnation of the "I" involves a particular crisis (*"I"-crisis*) at each stage (Bijloo, 2011, 199).

Childhood trauma disrupts the incarnation of the "I." As a result trauma victims develop "I"-*weakness*. When this happens, however, it is not the spiritual dimension of the "I" that is affected or disabled. Disturbances or damages that occur at the various levels of our organization prevent the "I" from carrying out its controlling and steering functions. The whole incarnation process is disrupted and the individuality is hindered or prevented from incarnating (de Raaf, 2011, 164f.):

- The phase of defiance we see in two-year-olds ("terrible twos") is the first manifestation of the "I." Children attain self-awareness in their thinking. Childhood trauma can weaken this "I"-awareness, placing afflicted children in danger of being flooded by all kinds of impressions and fears, leaving them feeling exposed and overwhelmed. The connection between "I" and body is weakened or even wholly disrupted.
- The second manifestation of the "I" occurs at around the age of nine or ten, during the "Rubicon crisis" (Steiner, 1979, CW 304, 47) when children experience themselves for the first time as separate from the world, this time in their feeling. This self-experience is important for the development of self-trust and a strong self-image (Selg, 2011a).

  Childhood trauma can diminish the "I"-experience and weaken the child's self-confidence. The resulting problems include a sense of isolation or problems with finding meaning

in life. The "I" is unable to establish a strong connection with its surroundings.
- The third time the "I" manifests noticeably is during adolescence, at around the age of 17. It is the time when the ideals of youth rise up and when young people can intuitively sense their prenatal motifs. During this phase of self-discovery the "I" awakes to its potential for self-actualization, for actively taking hold of one's own biography and making an impact in the world.

  Trauma can interfere massively with a young person's self-actualization and render the process of self-discovery difficult if not impossible. Trauma is always essentially an experience of helplessness, powerlessness, and inefficacy. "Fear, horror, helplessness, and loss of control are typical of such traumatic situations" (Morgan, 2007, 15).

When the inconceivable happens and trauma disrupts a person's life nothing will be as it used to be. The monster "trauma" corrodes the child soul. Traumatic events not only destroy the world outside; they can shatter a person's entire bio-psychosocial-spiritual organization. Trauma victims may lose contact with their environment and the connection with their own body. "Often we are not properly in our body after a traumatic event. Sometimes we unconsciously withdraw from our body because it is the place where the trauma resides" (Ibid., 77). Trauma disrupts the incarnation process and possibly the entire biography of the affected person.

Trauma Damages the Rhythmic System

Our body, soul, and spirit form a differentiated entity. Our spirit-soul and enlivened body relate to each other in a way that is conducive to physical and mental health. Trauma can damage or destroy this relationship.

Waldorf education takes account of the development and interaction of the child's soul, spirit, and body. Rudolf Steiner gave around

200 pedagogical lectures explaining the developmental psychology of Waldorf education. In all of these considerations the development of the child's spirit and soul is seen in connection with physical and physiological phenomena: "You must know that the children, while you teach and educate them, are busy with other things, too; they are growing. It is therefore important that your teaching and educating does not interfere with the child's growing. You must teach and educate in a way that can run parallel to the child's need to grow" (Steiner, 1992, CW 293, 167).

Rhythms are essential for our bio-psychosocial-spiritual dimension and development. Rhythm is part of life: "There are no life functions that don't recur in cycles or that don't have a certain rhythm or pulse; that don't breathe or alternate between phases of rest and activity" (Glöckler, 2006, 11). Where there is life there is rhythm. Over the last decades, chronobiological research has looked at the rhythms of plants, animals, and humans and discovered an abundance of rhythmical phenomena in almost all living organisms (Rosslenbroich, 1994, 15). The findings are particularly relevant in education, special education, medicine, and therapy. The rhythms in a child's organs, for instance, are not innate. "The younger a developing organism is the more it depends on the regular care and fostering of its biological rhythms. Such care will be rewarded in later life with strong health, adaptability, and stress tolerance" (Glöckler, 2006, 18). The endogenous organ rhythms are consequently only established in the early years of child development, triggered by the environmental rhythms of day, week, month, and year, which are guided by cosmic events and influences.

Endogenous Rhythms of the Organism

There are many rhythms in the human organism. We can divide them into three wider functional categories (Rosslenbroich, 1994)— the rapid shortwave rhythms of the nervous system, the more medium-wave rhythms of respiration and circulation, and the medium-wave to slow rhythms of metabolism and digestion (ibid., 41 ff.).

- The fast rhythms of the nervous system occur at split-second speed. The membranes of the nerve cells and sensory cells are designed for high-speed electrical potential changes, which are transmitted rapidly along neural pathways. Excitation frequencies of 1,000 per second have been verified. These excitations convey messages, and frequency is an important factor in this process. If a pain sensor in the skin is only slightly excited, the nerve impulse will travel along the neurons to the brain at a correspondingly slow tempo. The stronger the excitation the higher the frequency. "Sense impressions are consequently conveyed through the change of the excitation rhythm" (ibid. 35). The rhythms of the neurosensory system form the foundation of sense perception, conceptual processes, and other neural activity in the human organism. Stress can change, disrupt, or even destroy these rhythms.
- The slower rhythms of the metabolic system are the opposite of the fast neurosensory rhythms. They support the processes of nutrition and elimination and are much more stable as they possess frequencies of between a minute and an hour. The intestinal rhythm has a consistent pace of twelve per minute, while the peristaltic waves of the stomach that move the food on occur at a consistent frequency of three per minute. The rhythms of the gastrointestinal motor activity have a ratio of 4 to 1, corresponding to that of heart and respiration, and are related to the movement of the smooth muscle tissue that we also find in the blood vessels, the ureter, gallbladder, and the sexual organs. Wherever there is smooth muscle tissue in the organism we find a constant one-minute rhythm. Trauma can cause long-term damage to the rhythms of the metabolic system.
- The rhythmic system, which tends toward medium-wave frequencies, mediates between the two poles described above. The rhythmic system includes primarily heartbeat, respiration, circulation, and blood pressure but also motor activity. The

frequencies of the rhythmic system range from seconds to minutes. The blood circulation in the skin, for instance, changes at a rate of once per minute, exactly opposite the circulation in the muscles. If blood perfusion in the muscles is high, it is low in the skin. Their relationship changes rhythmically. "This system is not at all stable and breaks down in case of stress. Within limits, the rhythms can vary and adapt their frequency fluently to the prevailing demands" (Ibid., 43). The pulse–heart ratio of 4 to 1 is also a fundamental rhythmic principle of the human organism. While this relationship can vary individually depending on the demands experienced during the daytime, it is stable at night after a few hours of sleep. Rosslenbroich speaks in this context of "nocturnal normalization" (ibid., 27). "The need to establish a consistent rhythm is therefore one of the reasons why the organism needs to rest and regenerate during sleep.... This orderly rhythm is a prerequisite for genuine recovery. A test person who is woken from sleep every two hours will never achieve a heart-breathing ratio of 4 to 1 and their sleep will not be restorative" (Ibid., 27).

Sleep disorders and other rhythmic disturbances are typical symptoms of stress. As with the rhythms of the neurosensory and metabolic systems, traumatic experiences can massively disrupt the rhythms of the rhythmic system and lead to serious physical and mental health problems.

The Influence of Environmental Rhythms on Endogenous Rhythms

Many chronobiological studies show that, except for viruses and bacteria, all organisms have endogenous rhythms. These endogenous rhythms are superimposed and synchronized by nature or environmental rhythms. The tripartite system of endogenous rhythms in humans is also superimposed and entrained by the long-wave environmental rhythms of day and night, of the week, the month, the year, but also by longer rhythms such as the seven-year rhythm. The endogenous rhythms of the human organism are embedded in these external rhythms. Synchronization of endogenous rhythms and nature rhythms is triggered by pacemakers such as phases of light and darkness, temperature changes, or social triggers in a person's family or working life. These pacemakers trigger the organism's readiness to synchronize.

Within the human organism, the **circadian rhythm** with its phases of day and night manifests in our biological and mental energy, pain tolerance, the duration of medicinal effects, blood count, blood sugar levels, urine composition, the skin's cell division processes, and so on.

The **weekly rhythm** is apparent in disease processes, wound healing, and regeneration, in rejection processes after organ transplants, or in the adaptation to changes and stress. The weekly rhythm determines our working life as well as our cultural and religious life.

The **monthly rhythm** appears in the female menstruation cycle, in hormonal changes and uric acid levels.

The **yearly rhythm** also affects endogenous rhythms, with the seasons acting as cues—birth and mortality rates, seasonal disorder, immunity, blood levels, hormones, optical response times, physical strength, and much more.

Trauma Causes Desynchronization

The sensitive synchronization processes between the endogenous rhythms of the human organism and the rhythms of the environment are massively impaired by traumatic stress experiences. This impairment shows in a variety of rhythmical disorders and signs of desynchronization.

If the various endogenous rhythms of the human organism are no longer in harmony, this can lead to neurological movement disorders or dystonia. It can also happen that the endogenous rhythms are no longer in harmony with the environmental rhythms due to external desynchronization, as in the case of jet lag or shift work.

The synchronization of movement sequences is crucial for circus acrobats. When they perform their trapeze acts under the cupola of the circus tent, split seconds determine the success or failure of their act. It is similar with exogenous and endogenous rhythms. If they are not synchronized, a crisis situation arises within the organism, resulting in restlessness, sleeping problems, malaise, reduced performance, etc. Trauma can set off such a crisis. With behavioral disorders, the possibility of an underlying trauma always needs to be considered.

The Rhythms of Our Bio-Psychosocial-Spiritual Organization

The various levels of our bio-psychosocial-spiritual organization are also related through their rhythms. In a lecture presented in Berlin on 21 December 1908 and titled *Rhythms in the Human Organization*, Rudolf Steiner described those rhythms in detail (Steiner, 1988, CW 107, 148ff.).

The physical body develops at a yearly rate. Nine months of pregnancy plus three months during which the maternal antibodies continue to protect the infant's body against infection complete the period of time that the physical organization needs to become independent.

A monthly rhythm prevails in the life or ether body as we see in the case of healing processes after certain illnesses and of the menstrual cycle.

The soul or astral body carries our inner experiences. "The 'I' internalizes what it experiences in the world through sensations and feelings. This experience unites the 'I' with the world" (Schiller, 1992, 28). The soul or astral body has a weekly rhythm. "We notice a similarly subtle relationship, a swinging between inner and outer world, also in the week. As we pass through the days of the week, we experience subtle, scarcely perceptible, moods of soul excited by cosmic movements. These relationships are reflected in the names of the days of the week" (Ibid., 28).

The circadian rhythm governs the development of the individuality, the "I." "Through the day our human essence, or 'I,' keeps changing the degree to which it connects with the physical and life bodies. One could say the 'I' is present to varying degrees. Especially during sleep the 'I' withdraws, while it is especially strong when we are faced with challenges during the day. There are constant rhythmic changes in our 'I'-organization that determine our degree of consciousness" (Rosslenbroich, 1994, 129).

The "four levels of the human organization are interconnected and interdependent. They interact with each other in a very complicated way" (Steiner, 1988, CW 107, 149). Traces of the various rhythms of the human bio-psychosocial-spiritual organization can be found in all kinds of biological and physiological processes.

Trauma can cause long-term damage to the rhythms of the various levels of the human organization. A "shift" in their interaction can lead to psychopathological changes of consciousness.

Trauma Symptoms Vary with the Stages of Child Development

All mothers are familiar with the routine medical check-ups for children that determine whether and to what extent a child has attained certain age-specific developmental goals, because our biography unfolds according to particular laws and rhythms. Trauma can disrupt the rhythms of our organism and permanently damage the biographical rhythms.

As children grow up, their spirit and soul take hold of their physical and life body in three major developmental phases lasting seven years each (Lievegoed, 1995). In each of these developmental phases "the spiritual element which has connected itself with the body between conception and birth emancipates itself increasingly within the physical substance while it partly transmutes this physical substance into soul substance" (Windeck, 1984, 66).

Developmental Psychology Based on Anthroposophy

The first phase of child development extends from the physical birth to the age of seven. It is called the **first seven-year period** or early childhood. In these first seven years the child's body continues to be formed. When children leave the womb to be born, the different levels or members of their organization are "not equally mature" (Leber, 1992, 10). All four levels are present as we can see from the child's life processes, emotional manifestations, and the early forms of consciousness that appear in waking and sleeping. Body, soul, and spirit are clearly present, but the physical body is more mature than the other members are. According to Rudolf Steiner children inherit a "model body" from their parents and develop their physical structure from this model. But their organs, head, and brain in particular, still need to develop. Once the I has incarnated in the child it continues to use its inherent sculptural forces to shape and develop the organs (Ibid., 11).

In early childhood the soul is not yet sufficiently differentiated from the physical body. Young children are "all sense organ" (Steiner, 1991, CW 305, 18) and they develop by imitating their surroundings. "Children imitate what is going on around them and in the process of imitation their physical organs pour themselves into the forms provided for them" (Steiner, 1978, CW 34, 22).

When children reach the age of seven this formative process comes to completion; the skull, the central nervous system, and the sense organs in the head have ceased to grow. The change of teeth signals the end of this phase. "Once the second teeth have come through a particular growing or organizing power is no longer needed and is set free...to be used when the child enters school" (Steiner, 1979, CW 304, 77). "With the change of teeth, around the seventh year, we notice the power of imagination arising in the children. It has now become more or less individualized and is no longer tied to the body" (Ibid., 144). "We observe how the force that will be the child's thinking was previously a force of internal organic growth, and how this force of organic growth metamorphoses and appears as a soul force" (Steiner, 1998, CW 297a, 18).

Before the age of seven, children cannot think in abstractions. Their thinking is entirely pictorial. Children transform patterns of perception and activity into inner images. These images are imitations of the reality around them. This phase of childhood is mostly devoted to the full physical development of the neurosensory system as the foundation for mental and spiritual processes such as thinking.

According to the anthroposophic approach to education, children attain school maturity when the first seven-year period comes to an end. "When children reach school maturity the part of the ether body that is mainly linked to the nervous system is freed from the organic processes and serves the soul life as a foundation for thinking and remembering" (Schuberth, 1998a, 253).

With the **second seven-year period** or the middle of childhood (age seven to fourteen) abstract thinking emerges in a process that will reach completion only with the end of the third seven-year period. During this second phase, the child's rhythmic system matures—a process accompanied by noticeable changes in the soul life, because the soul "resides" in the rhythmic system. The child's feeling life changes because "feeling is not directly linked to our nervous system but to our rhythmic system, to the rhythms of respiration and circulation" (Steiner, 1991, CW 305, 51). Children of this age enter into a new relationship with their environment. For the first time they perceive a distance between themselves and others (Selg, 2011a, 17ff.).

Piaget based his developmental theory on similar phases, referring to this particular stage as "decentration" (Buggle, 1985, 80f.). "Children become increasingly able to objectify the thought processes which accompany their sense perceptions and to relate their own 'standpoint' to that of others, not only in their thinking, intentions and actions but, above all, socially" (Müller-Wiedemann, 1992, 86). Gradually the child's relationship to family members and to the teacher changes and grows into a mutually binding partnership. Children develop a growing sense of responsibility and an increasing awareness of right and wrong. Once respiration and heart rate are sufficiently mature, the final important stage of development begins.

With the **third seven-year period** or adolescence (age fourteen to 21) the young person's emotional life begins its journey of individualization.

Experiences such as pleasure and aversion, deliberate and involuntary actions, desires, and feelings, grow increasingly subjective in the young soul. Physiologically, this phase is governed by puberty, with metabolic and sexual maturation and intense skeletal growth. The young person is now capable of reproduction. Steiner speaks of "earth maturity" (Steiner, 1995, CW 317, 18).

Steiner associates this phase also with growing will forces because the heavier bones require enhanced will application for movement, balance, and the overcoming of gravity. In the newly awakened, purely physical, attraction of young people to the opposite sex Rudolf Steiner sees their increased capacity for love. If the young person develops in a healthy way, this capacity for love will mature into a profound interest in the world (Steiner, 1971, CW 302, 135).

For these new sentiments to become experiences, the young people need to penetrate them with their thinking. They need to develop intellectual awareness. Younger children do not reflect on their feelings, while adolescents need to question and evaluate theirs. Young people attain a level of understanding that allows them to form independent judgments and criticism. They realize that they can take responsibility for their own actions, feelings, and ideas (Staley, 1995; Köhler, 1990; Selg 2005).

With the end of puberty, the **fourth seven-year period** sets in at the age of 21. During this period the young adults achieve "social maturity"; they are now able to consistently and independently put into practice the certainty of judgment they gained during the third seven-year period (Leber, 1992, 13f.).

In the first three developmental stages we see the body, soul, and spirit merging and expressing themselves in thinking, feeling, and will. In each of the stages, one of the three soul forces prevails—thinking in the formation of the neurosensory system, feeling in the differentiation of the rhythmic system (breathing, circulation), and will in the maturation of metabolism and life processes. With each step the "I" develops further as the young individuality takes shape.

Within the context of the developmental stages it makes sense to mention the four members of the human organization again, which Steiner distinguishes as physical body, ether body, astral body, and "I." These members develop successively over the seven-year periods and appear as distinct layers of the human organization. Kayser compares them to a set of Russian matryoshka dolls: "The doll on the inside is the physical body. It is enclosed by the second doll, the ether body, which, in turn is enclosed by the third doll, the astral body. The outer layer, the fourth doll, corresponds to the 'I'" (Kayser, 1996, 14).

The pedagogical considerations that arise from this anthropological view form the foundation of Waldorf education and of Emergency Education. Trauma can have a lasting detrimental effect on the rhythms of child development.

The Effect of Trauma at the Various Stages of Child Development

The damage caused by trauma varies according to the stage of child development, because children's capacity for coping with trauma depends on their degree of biological, emotional, and social maturity. The specific symptoms we observe at the various stages of child or youth development reflect the corresponding physical-physiological, psychic-emotional, social, and cognitive coping mechanisms.

The following considerations are based on unpublished notes by the Israeli physician Meron Barak (Barak, 2006); during the first seven years of child development, traumatic experiences harm primarily the connection between life body (ether body) and physical body, affecting the metabolism-limb system in particular. It is therefore important that we foster and strengthen young children's basic senses of touch, life, movement, and balance by encouraging them to imitate and by introducing reliable rhythms.

In the second seven-year period trauma affects mainly the relationship of life body and soul (astral body) and the rhythmic system. All teaching ought to be imaginative and artistic during that time.

Eurythmy, painting, modeling, music, and all kinds of artistic activity will have a healing effect.

In puberty and adolescence, during the third seven-year period, trauma will most likely affect the relationship of the soul (astral body) and the individuality (the "I"), especially the neurosensory system. There is a danger of the astral body either not connecting sufficiently or entering too deeply into the metabolism-limb system. Social activities, clear thinking, and the occupation with ideals by studying biographies support healing at this stage of development.

Age-Specific Trauma Symptoms in Children and Adolescents

If trauma remains unresolved children develop age-specific symptoms depending on their physical, cognitive, emotional, and social maturity. The Hamburg pediatrician and child psychiatrist Andreas Krüger associates age-specific trauma experiences with Piaget's four stages of cognitive child development (Krüger, 2008, 50).

Impairment of brain maturation, immune system, self-regulation—prenatal child development; incidents that occur during the fetal period have a profound impact, since at that time the blueprint is created "that influences every system in the body from immunity to the expression and regulation of emotion, to nervous resilience, communication, intelligence, and self-regulatory mechanisms for such basics as body temperature and hormone production" (Levine and Kline, 2007, 34).

With infants who experience on-going stress, the brain that is still growing will focus on survival functions "at the expense of development in the limbic and cortical areas responsible for the regulation of impulse and emotion. The infant brain becomes hyper-alert to the perceived danger.... The brain becomes programed in such a way that feelings of terror and helplessness become a 'normal' state of being" (Ibid.).

These behavioral patterns manifest later, usually only when children have started school, in anxiety disorders, hyperactivity, attention deficit disorders, dissociation, depression, phobias, or behavioral problems. Infants who are threatened by violence in the first 33 months of their lives (including pregnancy) are likely to develop learning difficulties and abnormal behavior patterns: "Such children are predisposed to impulsive, violent behavior and/or mental disorders (such as depression and anxiety) due to the interactive experiences that shaped the brain during the critical period" (Ibid., 35).

The probability that former victims become perpetrators themselves in later life is very high: "Victims tend to become violent; male victims resort mostly to sexual and physical violence, female victims to emotional violence.... The soul development of children depends essentially on how they are treated" (Fietzek, 2006, 110).

Crying, Attachment Disorder, Failure to Thrive:
 The First Year of Childhood

> Sakuro is eleven months old and lives with his mother in a Japanese village near Fukushima. Since March 11, 2011, Japan's black day, he has exhibited an extreme startle response. Interspersed only with brief periods of sleep, he cries day and night and cannot be soothed. The mother who was severely shocked by the tsunami, has suffered from extreme anxiety ever since. She is close to a nervous breakdown.

Infants express trauma-induced distress in accordance with their physical, cognitive, emotional, and social maturity. They respond with severe motor restlessness. "Initial crying is accompanied by an increased startle response, diminished soothability, followed by sleeping disorders and feeding problems and a general failure to thrive" (Krüger, 2008, 51). Trauma caused by neglect, ill-treatment and abuse through an attachment figure will result in attachment disorders that may affect the ability to form relationships for the rest of a person's life (Ainsworth, 1978; Bowlby, 2001; Grossmann and Grossmann, 2003).

Krüger (2008, 50) lists the following age-specific posttraumatic stress symptoms:

- frequent crying
- increased startle response
- diminished soothability
- sleeping disorders
- feeding disorders
- general failure to thrive
- attachment disorders

Fears, Hyperactivity, Developmental Delay—Ages 1 to 3

> "All the children are terrified, especially when they see an airplane!" says Ebtesam Talmes (42), a mother of ten from Gaza. Somaya El Sultan (35), who has six children, adds, "My three-year-old son is even scared of birds. He wants to sleep all the time!"

Babies and infants have limited means of expression. They are vulnerable and unable to express verbally what happened to them. "Children who were maltreated in infancy can never put their harrowing experiences in words because they were not yet able to speak at the time. They did not memorize what happened as language but 'only' as emotional states" (ibid., 127). Babies and infants have other ways of communicating their trauma: "When babies and young children become overwhelmed, they may exhibit frantic distress reactions such as wailing, gasping, and flailing about. However, quite frequently, they instead shut down, constrict and 'go away.'... They simply detach or withdraw (the infant version of dissociation)" (Levine and Kline, 2007, 44).

Babies and infants are likely to present a variety of symptoms after a traumatic experience (ibid., 43), including fear, avoidance behaviors, increased irritability, withdrawal/shutdown, as well as impulsive behavior. Developmental delays and physical complaints such as stomachaches are also commonly seen.

Babies and infants frequently exhibit the following age-specific symptoms (Kocijan-Hercigonja, in Hilweg and Ullmann, 1998, 184f.):

- change of habits and behavior patterns
- regression to earlier stages of development
- frequent unexplained crying
- sleeping disorders
- eating disorders
- communicative disorders

Reenactment, Somatization, Regressive Behaviors—Ages 3 to 7

> Since the earthquake in 2010, all 53 children at Santo, an orphanage in a suburb of the Haitian capital of Port-au-Prince have been extremely anxious. They are afraid to live in a house. "They come to me in the night and lie close to me like cats. If I try to get up they cling to me," says Marie Jose, founder of Haiti Child Aid. The traumatized orphans suffer from constipation, diarrhea, eating, sleep, and memory disorders and febrile infections.

> Five-year-old Islam lost both his father and mother in an Israeli attack on Zeitoun (Gaza Strip) in 2009. Since then he has suffered from panic attacks, nightmares, night sweats, sleeping problems, social withdrawal, and stinging eye allergies.

Babies often respond to trauma by switching between protest and resignation. Kindergarten and pre-school children have a much wider range of coping mechanisms. "Common signs that young children have more feelings inside than they are able to manage are temper outbursts, tantrums, throwing toys, hitting or bullying siblings and playmates, biting, grabbing, and kicking" (Levine and Kline, 2007, 51). Other signs of excessive stress include "hyperactivity or numbing and shutdown, including withdrawal from play or from people, lethargy, and/or excessive shyness. This may alternate with bouts of inconsolable crying or tantrums. Traumatic stress might also show up as regressive behaviors to an earlier stage of development [sic]" (ibid., 46).

Traumatized children often feel caught in the traumatic experience. As a consequence they tend to be overexcited and reenact their trauma in play: "An overwhelmed youngster may funnel an energy overload (hyperarousal) into repetitive play that portrays some aspect of the traumatic event. This type of play lacks imagination and variety.... For example, you may notice your child repeating or reenacting one or more scenes or themes. This type of play appears to be driven almost out of desperation and does not seem to bring any satisfaction or relief" (Ibid., 47).

The syndrome of posttraumatic hyperarousal includes sleeping disorders (problems falling and staying asleep) and a noticeably increased startle response. If these symptoms become chronic they appear similar to those of ADHD. "High stress levels are normal for many children who later become conspicuous at school" (Fietzek, 2006, 114).

Intense emotional behaviors in children can also be a sign of helplessness. Posttraumatic stress symptoms include emotional outbursts as well as anxiety, fear, anger, aggression, and exaggerated protest. Many children also become very clingy after experiencing extreme distress: "Toddlers may express fearfulness by insisting on being carried or held constantly in an attempt to feel adult protection..." (Levine and Kline, 2007, 50f.).

If children keep asking questions, they might be afraid or distressed. Their questions "may be an attempt to maintain a sense of safety and control" (Ibid., 52).

Physical complaints can be symptomatic of trauma at all ages. These complaints may include digestive problems (diarrhea, constipation), stomach aches, a high temperature (also without infection), headache, but also shallow breathing with fatigue or lethargy due to limited oxygen flow to the brain (ibid., 53). Eating disorders are also common. Krüger summarizes the symptoms in children between the ages of three and seven as follows (Krüger, 2008, 50):

- fear
- tics (involuntary twitches)
- symptoms of dissociation
- somatization

- nightmares
- regressive behaviors (bed-wetting or soiling, thumb sucking, baby talk)
- reenactment of traumatic experiences
- regressive speech
- social withdrawal

Negative Outlook, Risky Behaviors, Depression: Children from the Age of 7 to 9

> Eight-year-old Issa lives in the Gaza Strip. In 2009 he lost his parents and siblings in an Israeli military attack. He keeps begging, stereotypically repeating the same words.

Traumatized children of early school age may exhibit signs of post-traumatic disorders such as lack of concentration or dissociative and learning disorders. Often, these children are plagued by intense feelings of guilt that they try to hide. As a result they develop symptoms of depression. Their general outlook grows ever more gloomy and pessimistic. "Children often adopt high-risk behaviors such as self-harming and cutting, they become suicidal or develop disorders formerly seen as 'conversive' such as psychogenic seizures, motor deficits or psychogenic behaviors" (ibid., 53). Compulsive behaviors are also common at this age.

Trauma symptoms often first emerge, or grow more pronounced, at school because children are exposed to greater intellectual and social pressure at school. The need to achieve and socialize can act as an additional stress factor. It is most important for teachers and educators "to spot symptoms of students with failure to cope, as well as to have the tools to intervene, before a major melt-down or violent acting-out occurs" (Levine and Kline, 2007, 55f.).

Trauma can manifest in many ways at school (ibid., 55). Traumatized children typically lack concentration or are disorganized and unable to finish set tasks. They may experience difficulties processing information or understanding what is asked of them. Their frustration tolerance is reduced, leading to sudden bursts of belligerence, aggression, or self-aggression. Due to chronic hyper-arousal children are fidgety and jumpy, have a shifty gaze and are easily distracted; they can't sit still, are hyper-alert and tend to interrupt and disturb lessons by talking non-stop. Fears and phobias are frequent, as are social withdrawal and shutdown (dissociation, isolation, extreme shyness, inattentiveness, fatigue, daydreaming, and depression). Tiredness, lethargy ("laziness") and a slumped posture are frequent manifestations of trauma.

Krüger (2008, 50) lists the following symptoms of posttraumatic stress for children aged seven to nine:

- impaired school achievements
- lack of concentration
- dissociation
- intrusive symptoms
- gloomy outlook
- sense of guilt
- symptoms of depression
- risky behavior
- self-harming
- suicidal tendencies
- psychogenic seizures
- motor deficiencies
- compulsive symptoms

EATING DISORDERS, REENACTMENT, SELF-HARMING BEHAVIORS: AGES 9 TO 14

Gregor has been a pupil at the Parzival School in Karlsruhe (Germany) since January 2009. Parzival School is a special school that offers educational support. Gregor had been excluded from several other schools because of considerable behavioral problems before he came to Parzival School. Especially after weekends it is almost impossible to teach Gregor in class. He tends to be over-excited and unable to stay in his place for any length of time. Or he is exhausted and slumps on his desk, sometimes fast asleep for hours. Gregor constantly interrupts the lesson, loudly commenting on anything the teacher says. It is his way of controlling what is going on in the lesson. His appearance and behavior reflect his inner state of chaos. He is provocative and humiliates and bullies weaker children. Outside school, Gregor spends much of his time playing Counterstrike. In school he stands out because of his verbal and physical aggression. Gregor displays criminal tendencies. He has been a regular smoker since he was 11 and consumes large amounts of caffeinated drinks. There are good reasons for believing that Gregor has been taking drugs for some time.

In autumn 2004 Gregor had been admitted to a specialist hospital near Heidelberg because of a rheumatic complaint. During his stay there he was abducted by a 30-year-old former member of staff who had previously been convicted of child abuse in 40 cases. Gregor's abductor locked him into a specially prepared wooden box. Three days later Gregor was found and freed by the police. He was covered in his own excrements and suffered from pneumonia. Gregor insists he only remembers two days of captivity. He denies the third day. For him the week of his abduction was the only week in the calendar that had only six days. "*It is the only week without a Friday!*"

Police investigations revealed that the abductor anaesthetized and abused some of his victims in a room that he had specially set up with medical equipment. He brought these children to the threshold of death and later reanimated them. Some of his crimes he recorded on video.

Young adolescents tend to have more resources than younger children do. Their linguistic and cognitive skills are more advanced and their social competence and sense of morality more highly developed.

School-aged children may display a variety of trauma symptoms (hyperarousal, avoidance, reliving, dissociation, contraction, freezing, etc.). In school children up to the age of 12 one observes symptoms such as flashbacks, physical reactions, problems with falling and/or staying asleep, phobias, aggression, inconsistent behaviors, etc.

Avoidance behaviors and signs of emotional numbness are more rarely observed in younger schoolchildren. These younger children tend to show trauma by talking about their experiences or by acting them out in play (Terr, 1995). They often suffer from unrealistic fears that they find very upsetting or they tend to believe in bad omens, thinking "that certain signs were warnings of the traumatic event that occurred and will reoccur. This is connected to the magical thinking of younger school-aged children" (Levine and Kline, 2007, 56). Superstitious beliefs, such as avoiding stepping on cracks in the pavement because it could bring bad luck, are very common among children up to the age of 12.

Schoolchildren also display details of distressing experiences in their traumatic play. Since their language skills are more advanced they tend to reenact their trauma by talking about it incessantly. But they are not able to verbalize their feelings. Their fears and total helplessness manifest in symptoms of hyper-arousal (they feel confused, overexcited, beside themselves, stunned) or disorganization.

Schoolchildren are more developed morally and are therefore able to think of others. When they re-live their trauma in narration they often focus, apart from the details of the traumatic event, also on their own role in it: "They may feel responsible and be plagued with feelings of self-blame or shame that they keep as a dark secret.... They think that if they had done something differently, the 'terrible thing' would never have happened" (Ibid., 56). Feelings of guilt are particularly frequent in situations that involve separation and they often result in the child's social alienation from family and friends.

Traumatic experiences can also change the vision school children have of the future. They often fear that "their future has been ruined, that they may no longer have anything to look forward to, or that they may not even have a future" (Ibid., 57).

Especially after sexual abuse children of this age tend to develop eating disorders, while other kinds of trauma may evoke self-aggression and suicidal tendencies. Excessive drug use is another frequent symptom: "With children who have experienced domestic violence, the expression of the traumatic event often shifts from the level of play to that of real relationships. The trauma, or traumatic event, is 'reenacted' socially" (Krüger, 2008, 53). There are many known cases of victims who feel compelled to seek out traumatizing situations. "Some trauma victims repeat their trauma all through their lives, again and again" (Morgan, 2007, 59).

Between the ages of nine and fourteen, schoolchildren tend to exhibit the following trauma symptoms (Kocijan-Hercigonja, in Hilweg and Ullmann, 1998, 184f.):

- worrying about others
- fear of trauma-relevant stimuli
- concentration problems
- memory problems
- learning difficulties
- compulsive reenactment of traumatic situations
- behavioral changes
- sleeping problems
- eating disorders
- somatic symptoms (e.g., stomach aches, headaches, palpitations)
- unwillingness to burden their parents with their problems

Drugs, Perversion, Fear of the Future: Adolescents from the Age of 14

Hitoshi (16) lost his family during the tsunami in Sendai. He is continuously overwhelmed by images of the disaster. *"He's like an inner tsunami!"* He constantly feels charged up. Hitoshi used to be a good pupil. His fears, concentrations problems, and states of excitement meant that he fell behind in school. The one thing that seems to help him is alcohol.

Adolescence is a crucial stage in a process of gaining autonomy that begins at the age of two and should find its conclusion with the end of adolescence. In this maturation process the individuality is formed, the ability to form relationships ripens and ethical values emerge. Overwhelming traumatic experiences can massively impair and disrupt this fragile and vulnerable process. "A lighthearted adolescence may be usurped by a premature and grim entrance into adulthood" (Levine and Kline, 2007, 67).

If the crucial symptoms of trauma (hyper-arousal, reliving, avoidance, dissociation, contraction, freezing, etc.) are discovered early enough they may be resolved quite easily. If they are neglected and the child is caught in a state of shock, she might develop "'secondary' symptoms weeks, months and even years later" (ibid., 67f.). In most cases the first symptoms manifest about four weeks after the traumatic event, but "with others the latency period lasts for years or even decades. In many instances, the reactions are triggered by seemingly insignificant events" (ibid., 69).

Young people who suffered violence in childhood are three times more likely to develop alcohol or drug problems than their peers. "Girls who showed internal trauma symptoms (withdrawal, depression, somatic disturbances) or external trauma symptoms (irritability, defiance, acting-out) had a higher incidence of substance abuse than girls who showed no symptoms; while for boys, only externalizing behaviors correlated with substance abuse. Those who themselves had been physically assaulted were twice as likely to suffer clinical depression; while sexual assault victims were 80% more likely to suffer from post-traumatic stress syndrome than other teens" (Ibid., 61).

While trauma symptoms in adolescence resemble those of adulthood, their long-term effects are different. Youngsters "tend to reexperience the events through flashbacks and make every effort to avoid activities, thoughts, and feelings that trigger recollection of the distressing events. If they do not dissociate the unpleasant memories, they will go to any length to numb out. For this reason it is common for traumatized teens to turn to drugs, alcohol, nicotine, sex, and dangerous thrill-seeking behavior as avoidance mechanisms to self-medicate and cope. They also tend to suffer more sleeplessness, irritability, depression, anxiety, and inattentiveness than their younger siblings" (Ibid., 61f.). Eating, sex, or music is also used as means for numbing out memories of distressing events. "Some kids may cut or otherwise injure themselves as a way to diminish their pain and, paradoxically, to get some control over their feelings" (Ibid., 62).

Traumatized youngsters soon fall behind at school and begin to exhibit defiant or challenging behaviors. As a next step they increasingly miss school or drop out altogether.

"When arousal energy...builds to an unbearable level, dissociation is the body's fail-safe mechanism that prevents a youngster from feeling like she is going crazy. It allows the compartmentalization of terrifying experiences from everyday reality....In this way, when painful reminders enter consciousness they can instantly be avoided—as though they don't exist" (Ibid., 63).

Lasting dissociation in adolescence, as happens in cases of long-term abuse by attachment figures, can result in dissociative identity problems and personality disorders.

Denial can also be seen as a mild form of dissociation. "Although the youngster is masked in a calm exterior, it is important to remember that she could actually be in a highly aroused state that is under the surface of conscious awareness. All it takes is a simple reminder, such as a sound, smell or even the season of the event, to blow the fragile cover and let loose the dam of sensations, thoughts, and feelings in a deluge...(Ibid., 64).

Levine and Kline provide a list of trauma symptoms frequently found in adolescence (ibid., 67):

- abrupt changes in relationships
- disinterest in formerly important relationships
- a sudden lack of interest in a once cherished hobby
- withdrawal, shutdown, isolation
- sudden behavior changes
- radical changes in life attitude, appearance, or school performance
- substance abuse
- sudden mood swings (fear, depression, suicidal tendencies)
- life-threatening acting out of the traumatic event
- increased irritability, anger, and aggression as well as a desire for revenge

Some youngsters seek out excessive sexual activity or keep changing their sexual partners as a result of their trauma.

This developmental phase as a whole is a "vicious circle of failure" (Krüger, 2008, 54) that is based on a distorted self-perception. "First intimate relationships fail due to destructive projections or exaggerated wishes for a symbiotic union. Substance abuse is frequent, especially involving cannabinoids and alcohol, both of which are particularly effective in case of intrusion and over-excitation. Even youngsters exhibit signs of sexual perversion in the aftermath of trauma and develop rigid, far-reaching fears of the future" (Ibid., 54).

The following list reflects trauma symptoms that may occur during adolescence (Kocijan-Hercigonja, 1998, 184f.):

- extreme behavioral disorders
- antisocial behavior
- irritability
- alcohol and substance abuse
- social withdrawal
- inability to envision the future
- changed values and attitudes about relationships
- suicidal tendencies

- other psychological disorders (psychoses, borderline personality disorder, depression)

There Are Many Ways of Becoming Traumatized

Trauma is caused by shocking events that leave the victims in fear for their lives and powerless to act.

> "I was in the teachers' room when the earthquake started. When I ran out I saw the whole disaster. Parts of the school had collapsed. Many pupils were caught under the debris, screaming for help. Injured children ran around aimlessly, crying. I was unable to speak, powerless, totally blocked. Everything around me seemed to turn and I was stunned. Someone sat me down on a chair. I didn't understand why I should sit down. I didn't realize the full scope of the catastrophe. I blame myself now because I wasn't able to help the children!" Thirty-five-year-old teacher Qiao Mingfeng from Yin Huong described her experiences after the severe earthquake on May 12, 2008. in the Chinese region of Sichuan. Her forty-five-year-old colleague Huongyou added, "When everything collapsed I couldn't see anything for all the dust. I felt my way forward, searching for children. Sometimes I touched heads, sometimes I saw only eyes. Many children were caught between lumps of concrete, unable to move, others were impaled by steel wire. One pupil clung to my leg. I did not recognize him. He kept screaming, 'It's me, teacher Huongyou! But I could not help him!'"

Trauma research classifies trauma either according to the type and duration of the violent impact or according to the situation surrounding the violent occurrence. In anthroposophic terms it makes most sense to differentiate between physical, sustained, verbal and relationship trauma. Physical trauma is caused by a one-off experience such as an accident, attack, medical intervention, natural disaster, and so on. Terr (1995) refers to such mono-traumas as type-I-trauma. Sustained trauma is the result of multiple traumatizations and is known as type-II-trauma. This category includes multiple traumatizations of different kinds as well as repeated traumatic experiences as in the case of ill-treatment, neglect, abuse, torture, or hostage situations. Verbal trauma

Devastation in the northwest of the Japanese island Honshu following the earthquake and tsunami of March 11, 2011

includes verbal aggression, mobbing, and bullying. Traumatic situations that involve bullying and mobbing can be highly complex. They belong to the category of psychosocial trauma (Hagemann, 2009, 78). Relationship trauma or traumatic stress in close relationships (neglect, ill-treatment, and abuse) severely affects the victim's whole biography, especially when inflicted in early childhood by an attachment figure. It can lead to severe, difficult-to-treat posttraumatic stress disorders or even suicide.

Natural disasters include earthquakes and landslides (earth), tsunami and flooding (water), hurricanes and tornados (air) and firestorms and lava streams (fire). All natural disasters belong to the type-I-trauma category. Among them earthquakes are particularly unsettling because the earth, our seemingly most reliable element, the foundation on which we literally build our lives, becomes unpredictable if not life threatening.

Trauma Means that the Soul Is Wounded

Wadi is 18 months old. He is one of the Samouni Clan, an extended farming family with over a hundred members that became sadly famous in December 2008, when Israeli troops marched into Zeitoun, a district in the southeast of Gaza City. The soldiers ordered clan members to gather in a house that was then shelled from a helicopter. Twenty-three members of the family, including many children, died. For four days the rescue teams of the Red Crescent were prevented from seeing to the injured victims and retrieving the dead (Melzer, 2010, 298 ff.). Wadi lay next to his dead mother during all that time. From time to time soldiers would pour a bucket of cold water over him. Wadi has not spoken since. His empty gaze cannot focus on anything. With his dark, unseeing eyes he looks into the world.

Soul Wounds Can Be Infectious

A wounded soul is like a wounded body. The boundaries of either organism are damaged. What used to be inside pours out. There is pain that wants to come to expression. The process of wound healing occurs in stages and may be hindered by a number of complications. Wounds may become infected due to a lack of hygiene or wound care and, as a result, inflammation, suppuration, even blood poisoning may occur in which case medical help is needed. In rare cases the situation may become life threatening for the victim.

With trauma the healing process follows a regular pattern, too, but this regularity can also be disrupted by complications. After the initial phase of shock, usually lasting a day or two, various symptoms may develop. Apart from a variety of psychosomatic responses (allergies, headache, indigestion, a weakened immune system, etc.), victims may have a distorted experience of space or time or develop perceptual disturbances. Trauma symptoms may include amnesia or compulsive flashbacks, paralysis or hyperactivity, depression or aggression, fear, panic, nightmares, concentration problems, withdrawal, sleep or eating disorders, feelings of guilt or shame, loss of self-respect, and many others. Victims will do anything to avoid thoughts, sensations,

*A young member of the Samouni family
among the ruins of war in Gaza, July 2009*

meetings or places that might remind them of the disaster. Many feel inwardly frozen, numb, or empty. The parts of the human fourfold organization have become loosened, and thinking, feeling, and will dissociate. "Some people 'beam' themselves out of the traumatic situation" (Morgan, 2007, 16). Trauma victims come close to the threshold; they may have panoramic views of their lives or similar experiences known from near-death research (van Lommel, 2009).

A traumatic shock is a partial death experience. With around 75 percent of earthquake victims, symptoms gradually subside and disappear after four to eight weeks. If symptoms persist beyond that time we speak of posttraumatic stress disorder, with each symptom potentially developing into a separate illness. Trauma can sometimes be masked by depression, fears, addictions, or self-destructive behaviors. Physical symptoms or suicidal thoughts are other possible signs of an underlying trauma (Morgan, 2007, 57ff.). Posttraumatic stress disorder (PTSD) is one of the most common consequences of trauma and requires treatment. Statistically, around 25 percent of the earthquake victims in Northern Japan will develop PTSD.

Victims Can Become Perpetrators

> Almesa and Zenab, two 13-year-old girls from the Samouni family, were also victims of the attack in Zeitoun, Gaza (Melzer, 2010, 298ff.) Buried under the ruins of the house, Almesa clung to her dead parents for four days. She speaks about the experience, describing how she gathered all her strength to chase away the rats that had started to eat the corpses. When asked about her future, she says tearfully "When I grow up I will join the armed brigades and kill the people who murdered my family!"

Trauma sufferers who are not able to work through their experiences may undergo profound and permanent personality changes. Victims who reach this chronic stage can feel constantly under threat. Often they respond with hostility, aggression, resignation, or depression. They tend to become socially isolated. Relationships fail; they lose their jobs; what used to be valuable becomes meaningless. Addictions and criminal tendencies may result. A person's biography threatens to break apart and the victim becomes a perpetrator. The war experiences of children in Gaza will, if they remain unresolved, provide fertile soil for a new generation of suicide bombers.

Posttraumatic stress disorders do not necessarily evolve in the four stages described above. Symptoms may subside after a while, so that it appears as if the experience has been resolved and integrated. Yet, weeks, months or years, even decades later the symptoms can erupt again and lead to posttraumatic disorders.

When the State of Alarm in the Brain Cannot Be Deactivated

Trauma can lead to long-term neurological changes. According to recent findings, very young children whose conscious memory is not yet developed are particularly at risk. The reason for this lies in the malleability of the human brain, also referred to as neuroplasticity. Nerve cells can change and adapt. The more often they are activated the stronger and denser they grow. Their ability to establish contact with other nerve cells is enhanced and close synaptic connections or neuronal networks are formed. If these networks are not used the links between them degenerate and disappear.

We memorize sense impressions, thoughts or newly formed concepts together with the emotional context in which we experienced them. The neural processes and pertinent emotions remain inscribed in our memory as an inseparable entity. We never remember bare facts. Learning processes can therefore be enhanced if they are associated with intense feelings because the combination of the two strengthens the neuronal networks. The process is the same for positive as well as negative feelings. Extreme trauma is coupled with emotions that will root the traumatic experience deeply in the victim's long-term memory.

Modern brain research has revealed how very sensitively the brain of the growing child responds to stress, especially during the first three years of infancy. Trauma can cause disruptions in the processing of neuronal information that cannot be corrected. The earlier or more frequently children experience threatening or violent behavior, and the more intense these experiences are, the more deeply functional changes will imprint themselves in the children's thinking, feeling, and behavior, causing abnormalities (Perry, 2003, 25). This also applies to the first three years of infancy when the neuronal foundations for conscious memorization are only just being established. Even though infants are not yet able to store away conscious memories of emotionally disturbing events, their body will remember them and set into motion the corresponding physiological responses.

> Svenja (12;7) is in class 6 at the Parzival School in Karlsruhe, a special school that bases its approach on the principles of Waldorf education (Reveriego and Ruf, 2000; Reveriego, 2001). Svenja reacts with panic, fear, and blind aggression when her teacher wears a jumper with a particular pattern. She behaves as if her life was in danger. Svenja cannot explain her reaction or give reasons for her violent emotional outbursts. She has no memory of a particular event but something triggers her flashbacks. Following traumatization, almost anything can be such a trigger—places, colors, smells, sounds, movements. Sometimes a gaze is enough to bring back a disastrous experience from the past.

Many Japanese children who survived the tsunami never flush the toilet because the sound of the running water triggers flashbacks of Japan's "black day." Flashbacks are horror films. They are not ordinary memories that can be differentiated into past and present events. A person who has flashbacks relives the disaster—however long ago it may have happened—as immediately and intensely as if it was happening again and is overwhelmed by the same fears, emotions, and physical or physiological reactions.

> Ahmet (13;1) is at the same school as Svenja. He comes from Afghanistan where he witnessed the killing of many members of his family during the war. At the school he attended in a Pakistan refugee camp he was constantly disciplined during lessons by a teacher who smashed his right arm by hitting it with a club. Ahmet has developed severe school phobia. He talks to himself continuously.

Ahmet's ongoing monologue can be seen as his unconscious attempt to heal himself. He has developed a defense strategy that helps him to suppress the tormenting flashbacks. Experts speak of avoidance behavior in victims that "can be so extreme that they are unable to lead a normal life" (Morgan, 2007, 57).

Our organism has an alert and defense system, referred to as a "stress axis" by scientists, that extends from the head to the adrenal

Psychological Trauma

A drawing by a child from the Sendai region in Japan, showing a person being carried away by a giant wave (one of the emergency education activities carried out by the Friends of Waldorf Education between April 27 and May 10, 2011)

glands. Within this biological early warning system, the limbic system, a set of structures located in the middle of the brain that is involved in memory as well as in emotions related to survival, takes up a central role. As soon as the amygdalae, which are part of the limbic system, register a threatening situation through monitoring the sum total of sensory stimuli, a rapid biochemical chain reaction is put in motion (Hüther, 2002). Stress hormones such as adrenaline, noradrenaline and other messenger substances are released quickly. The organism is prepared for a biological emergency program that is rooted in the human brain stem and decides between attack behavior (fight) or defense behavior (flight). If both responses seem impossible or if the impact of the stress experience is so strong that the organism is overwhelmed or blocked by it, a third behavior pattern, that of feigning death, can be activated. The victim freezes, like a terrified rabbit before a snake or a shy deer in the headlights of a car. The effectiveness of the cortex, the youngest part of the "triune brain" (Levine and Kline, 2007, 86), that is associated with rational thinking, problem solving and planning, is reduced, disconnected, or disabled. The fight, flight, or feigning death responses are survival mechanisms of the organism in life-threatening situations. If this high-alert state does not stop once the danger is over, the corresponding neuronal networks are enhanced at the expense of other synaptic connections. Brain functions are transformed and the organism remains in a permanent state of alert. Persons affected feel they are constantly in danger of losing their lives. They are in a "state of high alert but the energy generated by this is not used" (Morgan, 2007, 15).

As the brain develops in childhood, the more highly evolved brain areas of the limbic system, and later of the cortex, increasingly take charge of and change the more primitive and more reactive areas of the brain stem. This cerebral maturation can be massively and irreversibly disrupted by early-childhood trauma. Once the cortical control is lost, excitation levels will invariably rise and lead to an increase in impulsiveness, aggression, and hyperactivity.

As a result traumatized children process sensory stimuli in an unusual way. They have difficulties understanding verbal information. Instead they place too much value on non-verbal signals, which they often misinterpret. "Victims see eye contact as a threat; a friendly hug is interpreted as a preliminary stage of seduction and rape.... Cut off from the internal regulation of the cortex, the brain stem responds to any perceived threat with reflexes, aggression, and impulsive behavior" (Perry, 2003, 45f.).

Thanks to new imaging techniques, neuroscience has in recent years contributed much toward a better understanding of the origin of trauma and the process of traumatization. The changes in neuronal networks and central brain functions reveal the profound biological consequences the experience of trauma can have. The anthropology that underlies Waldorf education sees the brain as a "mirroring device." Our brain does not produce thoughts or mental images, but mirrors the suprasensory activity of life (ether) body, astral body, and "I." Through this mirroring process we achieve consciousness (Steiner, 1977, CW 129, August 24, 1911). Thoughts and memories are formed in our ether body. The brain merely mirrors them (Steiner, 1958, CW 138, August 26, 1912).

Trauma Does Not Necessarily Lead to Posttraumatic Disorders

> Carolin (18) was 16 when, on 11 March 2009, an attacker caused a bloodbath among pupils and teachers at Albertville School in Winnenden, Germany. Sixteen bullets hit Carolin's best friend Steffi who sat next to her. "The girls had swapped places on that morning, for no particular reason. But it saved Carolin's life while Steffi was killed" (Donowitz and Lache, 2011, 81). It seems almost incredible, but Carolin did not need trauma therapy after the horrific attack. She felt annoyed by the questions of the crisis intervention team and refused to see a psychologist. But Carolin did not suppress her horrifying experiences. She thinks of Steffi every day. The conversations that helped her resolve the trauma took place within her family and circle of friends. "The girl has an amazing emotional shield" (Ibid., 81). To this day Carolin does not display any signs of PTSD, with one exception; she never sits with her back to the door. "Her mother wonders if at some point, in five or ten years' time, the memory of this awful morning will surge up in Carolin and overwhelm her" (Ibid., 81). Such a turn of events is possible but not inevitable.

Many people experience the unthinkable. Some work through their trauma, others suffer till the end of their lives. Statistically, PTSD affects approximately 15 percent of accident casualties and patients with severe organ disease, 25 percent of people who experienced violence, and 50 percent of victims of war, imprisonment or displacement, rape or abuse (AWMF, March 30, 2007). Sexual abuse, neglect, and maltreatment by an attachment figure cause severe posttraumatic stress in almost 100 percent of affected children. Symptoms include bipolar disorder, dissociative personality disorders, and other disorders on the bipolar spectrum, delinquency, or other psychopathological illnesses. Trauma research is still trying to work out why the victims of disasters, natural or human-caused, and those of human tragedies respond so differently to extreme stress.

Stressors, Mediators and Stress Response:
  A Stress Model in Search of an Explanation

In 1987, the American stress researcher Leonard Pearlin presented a quite complex interdisciplinary stress model that depicts stress as a process. Aside from mental and social factors, the model includes the socioeconomic context as one of many factors involved in the emergence of stress-related health problems. The stress process can be roughly divided into three components (Pearlin, 1987):

- **Stressors**, or bio-psychosocial conditions that cause stress. They include anything a person may perceive as a threat. This could be a critical life situation (separation, illness, change of work place, moving to a new house) that requires adaptation to a new environment. The more drastic this change the greater the resulting stress and the higher the health risk. Unwanted, unexpected, or uncontrollable life events in particular have high stress potential. Ongoing difficulties, on the other hand, can also evoke stress reactions due to their permanent impact (marital problems, worries at the work place, difficult parent–child relationships).
- **Mediators** are safety or risk factors that either attenuate or augment the impact of stressors. Mediators can be of a personal or social nature. Personal mediators include resources such as individual coping mechanisms or strategies, behavioral dispositions, self-confidence, etc. as well as the ability to mobilize social support networks. Like personal resources, the social mediators also act as buffers. Being embedded in a

social network of relationships with attachment figures can help people deal with challenging social circumstances, critical life events, or chronic stress.
- **Stress responses** occur at all organic levels. Psychosomatic responses tend to manifest first after stressful experiences. They are somato-physiological malfunctions that may come to expression in long-term organic illness or damage.

Pearlin's stress model is based on the view that we are not passively exposed to environmental stress but that we are agents who deal actively with external influences. Life crises, chronic stress, disadvantageous life situations might be difficult to alter but we are only partly at the mercy of such stressors. We have the possibility to cultivate personal and social resources, which will then be available to control stress responses and avoid damage to our health. This is relevant for preventative and intervention strategies; there are buffer effects in stress situations that we can individually control. The effect a stressful event has on us depends not only on the event itself but also on the way we deal with it!

Trauma Is Caused by Extreme Stress

Trauma results from extremely stressful events. The psychological response to trauma is directly related to the traumatic event. However, there are many more factors that may affect the trauma process and co-determine whether someone can cope with a stressful event or develops PTSD. "A variety of factors such as lack of social support, the presence of additional problems in life, the severity of the trauma, a difficult childhood, or low intelligence emerged as particularly important risk factors. These variables explain why not everybody who experiences trauma will develop long-term psychological problems" (Landolt, 2004, 55).

Safety factors are factors that promote and enhance trauma resolution. A protected childhood, reliable caregiving by at least one attachment figure, physical and mental health, as well as stress tolerance and intelligence are important safety factors that help cope with stressful events. Additional factors that support trauma resolution and help to avoid posttraumatic stress disorders include self-assurance, religious beliefs, a network of friends, education, and openness about the traumatic event.

Risk factors are factors that hinder or impede trauma resolution. Previous trauma, stress, low self-esteem, illness, poverty, the lack of social support through family and friends, adverse childhood experiences, drug addiction, and low intelligence can detrimentally affect the trauma process.

But whether or not someone develops PTSD also depends on how the stressful event affects them, how they look at it, how much significance or meaning they attach to it. Children are not neutral toward a traumatic event; they interpret and assess the process. This assessment affects their bio-psychosocial situation that explains why comparable traumatic events can evoke a variety of responses. "Whether or not an event results in trauma depends particularly on how children interpret and classify this event. The subjective classification processes...are shaped by features pertaining to the trauma (kind of trauma), to the child (age, personality) and to the environment (parental response to the trauma)" (Landolt, 2004, 59). All these features can act as either safety or risk factors.

The external threat is consequently only one of several factors involved in the trauma process. The child's resilience is another crucial factor (Levine and Kline, 2010, 22). Aside from the actual event, the victim's subjective experience and assessment of the event play an important part. Whether an experience is traumatic for a child and whether the child develops PTSD depends mainly on the child's resources in coping with the stress situation.

Salutogenesis and Resilience: What Keeps Us Healthy in Spite of It All

Aaron Antonovsky's (1997) answer to the question of mental health in the face of adversity in life was his concept of "salutogenesis." According to this concept, mental health essentially depends on three factors that allow us to develop an inner sense of mental coherence (Niemeijer, 2011c, 141). He refers to these three factors as comprehensibility, manageability, and meaningfulness.

The first prerequisite for coherence is the child's fundamental trust that the internal and external world is structured, predictable, and explainable (comprehensibility). Children need to feel that they understand what is going on.

The second prerequisite for coherence is the child's fundamental trust that the life events, including trauma, can be managed. Self-abandonment considerably increases the risk of posttraumatic disorders such as PTSD. Children need to be able to trust that they can cope with a situation.

The third prerequisite for coherence is the child's fundamental trust that the demands of life are meaningful challenges or tasks that merit an active effort and commitment (meaningfulness). Children need to feel that events are meaningful. Viktor Frankl (2008) also sees meaningfulness as a crucial factor in health preservation.

The three pillars that support coherence are crucial safety factors in trauma management. When the external stress experiences outweigh the coherence factors, victims become overwhelmed by the stressful event. Their sense of coherence, and therefore their mental health, break down and they are in danger of developing PTSD.

Inner mental coherence belongs to the level of the "I." Our "I" processes experiences and integrates them into our biography. The "I" regulates the impulses and emotions of our soul life. These "I"-functions reduce our susceptibility to mental disorders and the incidence of PTSD.

3

Emergency Education

Bringing Healing to Injured Souls

When if Not Now?

It all started during the 2006 World Cup, when Stuttgart, in Southern Germany, was playing host to some of the football matches. The city's mayor organized a cultural "fringe" program and invited 2,006 young people from all over the world to a UNESCO Peace Festival. Being well aware that Stuttgart was not only famous for Porsche, Mercedes, and Bosch but also for the Waldorf school movement—the first Steiner Waldorf school opened here in 1919 and has since grown into a worldwide movement with schools in over 80 countries—he also invited 300 Waldorf pupils from 16 nations. The Friends of Waldorf Education, a support organization of the international Waldorf school movement, were asked to take on the planning, organization, and management of this event. When the World Cup was over, the Waldorf school in Überlingen, a town south of Stuttgart, invited the Waldorf youth of the world to a weeklong conference at Lake Constance. This educational peace celebration was in full swing when the Israeli–Lebanese War broke out. Lebanon's infrastructure was severely damaged in the Israeli air raids; airports, bridges, and main traffic arteries were destroyed and the Southern parts of the country temporarily occupied by Israeli troops. Twenty-one students from the Beirut Waldorf School—the only group of disabled youngsters to attend the Stuttgart UNESCO Peace Festival—could not return home.

The Lebanese youth group found a friendly host and a welcoming home in the Karl-Schubert School, a special needs Waldorf school in Stuttgart, and the City Council spared neither effort nor expense to provide an entertaining program for the involuntary visitors. The German organizers were happy to be able to offer the young people from Lebanon a safe place to stay, thinking that being far away from the crisis back home would be best for them.

But their view was not shared by the Lebanese partners who urged that the young people return home. Their families implored the bewildered German organizers to do all they could to send the group back home as soon as possible. The young people began to respond to the tenseness of the situation by displaying increasing stress symptoms characteristic of their particular disabilities. This conflict situation in Stuttgart had arisen as a result of different cultural values and traditions; Lebanese families tend to move more closely together if their lives are in danger, potentially even so they can die together.

In the end, the project organizers in Stuttgart and the Friends of Waldorf Education decided to comply with the wishes of the Lebanese families and send the disabled youngsters back to Beirut—into the war zone! Following detailed arrangements with the Lebanese authorities and Israel's military leadership and equipped with a letter of protection from UNESCO, the young people set off on an adventurous two-day journey home via Syria and Northern Lebanon. In Beirut they were handed over to their delighted parents. Their German travel companions were later received and honored by the Lebanese President and the "repatriation" was widely reported on in the Southern German and Lebanese media.

What the media did not mention was that the German helpers experienced something first-hand that they had previously only known from television—war. In the refugee camps they met the human victims, the "collateral damage" of the political interests—traumatized children, disturbed, pale, apathetic, bereft of their childhood, their gazes empty and dull. Any special or curative teacher will know that, in the early stages of trauma, it is relatively easy and effective to help traumatized children to resolve their trauma. They know also how difficult this will be at a later stage when the trauma symptoms and responses have become chronic. Teachers and therapists, who look at these children's eyes, know what needs to be done.

The traumatized refugee children at the Beirut Waldorf School inspired the impulse for an "emergency education in crisis situations" based on the principles of Waldorf education.

Psychosocial Support Is First Aid for the Child's Soul

> In a shelter in Zeitoun in the Gaza Strip, 12-year-old Mahmoud, who is severely traumatized, receives emergency education, next to a sick donkey. "Soldiers with tanks shot at us with smoke. My sister was lying on the road; she was hurt. Two helicopters circled above her. Many people fled. Lots of dead bodies were lying at the petrol station. My sister's son is dead, her husband is dead, another of her sons is injured. I can no longer concentrate at school!" Mahmoud had become conspicuous because of the extreme brutality depicted in his drawings.

Trauma changes the lives of children profoundly and lastingly. Children who have been through a traumatic event need special support and affection. Alongside psychological methods, the concept of using educational approaches to overcome trauma has been developed in recent years. "Trauma education sees itself as a (special) educational approach that aims at stabilizing and supporting traumatized children and youngsters" (Kühn, 2009, 26).

The **holistic stabilization** of traumatized children comprises four levels and is a crucial foundation for any therapeutic interventions that might be required later (Landolt, 2004, 88; Hausmann, 2006, 92ff.). The four levels are:

- **Physical stabilization.** The first essential step in emergency education is to make the affected children feel safe. For this they need a place where they feel physically safe. The children need

Emergency Education

Tears of joy at a reunion in Beirut, Lebanon, August 2006, following the successful journey home of 21 Waldorf students

to reconnect with their own (physical) body. It is therefore a priority that any physical injuries or ailments receive medical attention.

- **Somatic stabilization.** The functions of the life or ether body need to be supported and strengthened so that the etheric wounds and injuries can heal and congestions and blockages be dissolved. This allows children to experience their body again as a whole entity and a place where they can feel safe and develop a sense of continuity.
- **Psychosocial stabilization.** Reliable networks of relationships need to be established that can convey protection and safety. Establishing relationships means building up the necessary trust in the environment in order to strengthen the child's soul or astral body. Especially when children are severely

traumatized or suffer from comorbid disorders, it is essential that they are psychologically stabilized before any trauma therapies are attempted. Suitable methods of stabilization at this level include artistic educational approaches such as painting, drawing, modelling, play and drama; movement (sports, walking, gymnastics, eurythmy); resource-based processes (diary techniques, body-oriented techniques, imaginative techniques, etc.) and behavioral therapy (anxiety-management, assertiveness training, etc.) The overall aim is to strengthen children's weakened self-esteem in relation to their environment.

- **Mental-biographical stabilization.** Trauma can cause developmental retardation or blockages and destroy the victims' confidence in their ability to shape their own biography. The reason for this is that the human essence (the "I") is prevented from incarnating in the right way. Mental-biographical stabilization means that negative traumatic experiences are corrected or replaced by positive life experiences. It encourages trauma victims to actively take hold of and shape their life again.

Psycho-educational instruction has also been effective at the psychosocial level of stabilization, but it needs to be age-appropriate if used for children. Trauma victims who understand what trauma is, how it evolves and how it may manifest, will suffer less physically and mentally and are not in danger of thinking of themselves as mentally ill.

Emergency Education Is Not Trauma Therapy

Trauma can be treated in many different ways. "It is always about healing wounds. The greatest danger is that one might open up the wound again without being able to staunch it" (Donowitz and Lache, 2011, 78).

The educational, psychological, or therapeutic interventions chosen depend, among other things, on the stage of the trauma process.

As a rule, the first intervention needed by children who are in acute shock or in the subsequent phase of posttraumatic stress is the psychosocial stabilization described earlier. Therapy is only necessary if there is an illness that needs treating. Trauma therapy that helps traumatized children to process their stress experiences is therefore usually only introduced weeks after the phase of posttraumatic stress when an actual illness becomes apparent. Trauma therapy confronts victims with the traumatic event that they are trying to suppress. The therapeutic process enables them to resolve the trauma and integrate it in their biography. Therapy that is introduced too early can undermine the natural healing process. The soul wound is reopened and the trauma therapy itself can become a new trauma by aggravating what it ought to alleviate.

Emergency education is not trauma therapy. Its educational-artistic methods, which are based on the principles of Waldorf education, are applied in the first weeks after the traumatic event but before the stage of posttraumatic stress sets in. Emergency education seeks to activate and strengthen the child's powers of self-healing in order to prevent, or at least assuage, pathological developments.

Traumatized Children Need Places of Safety

Malalak is a mountain village in West Sumatra. The headmaster of the village school, Kaidir Zein, speaks of conspicuous trauma-induced behaviors among his pupils after the severe earthquake that shook the area in November 2009: "Many children are aggressive and hyperactive during the day. They are defiant toward their parents and teachers. But as soon as it gets dark they are very frightened. They are afraid of falling asleep or they wake up in the night crying, haunted by nightmares." Aggression and fear are typical responses to trauma. The teachers in Malalak speak of concentration problems, lack of motivation, and growing discipline issues: "They no longer listen to the teachers but run around the room during lessons, shouting and ignoring us." When the Emergency Education team arrives, headmaster Kaidir Zein asks if they have brought presents since,

Laughing children holding a handmade doll, West Sumatra, Indonesia, following the earthquake of November 2009

without, they wouldn't have a chance of "motivating the children to work." Astounded, he stands shortly afterward in a big circle with 130 children. All of them had stayed behind after school, voluntarily, to join in with games and other activities. "You got the children to laugh again, you opened up their hearts and made their eyes shine," is how Kadir Zein summed up his impressions at the end of the day.

Before any trauma therapy can be attempted trauma victims have to feel safe again. This sense of safety can be established with special imaginative exercises that start by evoking beautiful, empowering inner images. Such imagination techniques help to build up inner places of safety to which trauma victims can retire when flashbacks threaten to overwhelm them. The inner images are like safe anchorages in a harbor that protect the boats from being swept away by the surging waves of the ocean.

Based on these considerations, trauma therapist Luise Reddemann developed the concept of "psychodynamic imaginative trauma therapy" (PITT) (2008). Reddemann encourages trauma victims to imagine the parts of their inner life that have been hurt by the traumatic experience and then asks them to take these parts to an imagined place where they are cared for, nurtured, and healed by imagined helpers. Andreas Krüger, a psychiatrist at the trauma clinic of the university hospital in Hamburg-Eppeldorf (Germany) developed Reddemann's concept further and adapted it for children (Krüger and Reddemann, 2007).

Both Reddemann's and Krüger's approaches to trauma therapy are derived from the "ego states model" developed by the American psychologists Helen and John Watkins (Watkins and Watkins, 2003). According to this thought model we combine within ourselves the most diverse "ego states," such as the role of the son, husband, father, brother, professional roles, the role of victim and perpetrator, and so on. "When people suffer injuries to their soul they develop, as a kind of defense mechanism, new ego states; they segregate these severely injured states and lock them away in an inner dungeon. But from this dungeon the ego-states unfold a destructive life of their own which can soon dominate the whole personality." Through trauma therapy these segregated and repressed "parts of the self" can be reintegrated into the overall personality.

Emergency education also strives to build spaces of both objective external protection and subjective inner safety. Trauma sufferers need a protected, reliable place so they can begin to feel safe again. It is the only way for children to reestablish the connection with their natural environment and with other people that was destroyed by the trauma.

It is equally essential for the further development of traumatized children that they can reconnect to their own bodies. The body must become a place of safety again, a safe home for the child's spirit-soul. In order to achieve this one needs to nurture the senses, especially the sense of touch. Our skin forms the boundary between the inner and outer world. The skin delineates and protects inside and outside and mediates between the two. The sense of touch resides in the skin. Experiences of touch allow us to feel the world around us, ourselves, and our own boundaries. The sense of touch gives us the experience of our own body. Inside this body we can feel safe (König, 1986, 12ff.). Wounds violate this boundary. Physical contact—if the child allows it—such as stroking, holding, rhythmic *Einreibung*,[1] massaging, baths and compresses, enhanced body awareness, and reconnecting children with their body.

At the same time, traumatized children have been particularly sensitized to sensory stimuli. The trauma-induced lack of sensory integration makes it difficult for them to cope with external stimuli. Commotion, noise, traffic, exposure to visual or acoustic media, being confronted with too many objects—all of these will soon lead to a sensory overload that, in turn, causes over-excitation, fears, and hyperactivity. Protecting traumatized children from excessive external stimulation will also help them to reestablish a healthy connection with their own body so that it can become a safe place again.

For children to feel safe in their body it is also necessary to nurture their life processes. These processes are closely related to our life or ether body. We best nurture the child's life processes by offering a healthy, balanced diet, by fostering the child's biological rhythms and warmth organism, by teaching children about hygiene, by providing a safe place for sleeping and, above all, by giving love and affection. All this will help children to reconnect with their body. Emergency education helps to create external and internal places of safety.

---

1. "Rhythmic Einreibung" is a therapy of rhythmic body oiling. Its techniques were developed by Dr. Margarethe Hauschka on the basis of suggestions from Dr. Ita Wegman, founder of the clinic in Switzerland that bears her name. Dr. Wegman trained in Swedish massage, and rhythmic Einreibung is a development of this technique that emphasizes rhythmic elements and qualities to create lightness rather than pressure. The strokes work with the surface of the skin rather than kneading the body as is done with conventional massage techniques (Monika Fingado, 2011).

EMERGENCY EDUCATION IS PART OF TRAUMA EDUCATION

Emergency education applies methods that provide stability for traumatized children. It is introduced at a stage when it becomes apparent whether a child will cope with the trauma or develop posttraumatic disorders. Emergency education is therefore not trauma therapy in the classical sense. Emergency education seeks to activate and strengthen the powers of self-healing in trauma victims, whether they are children, adolescents, or adults. Its educational-therapeutic interventions are based on the principles and the anthropology of Waldorf education. Emergency education can help to stabilize traumatized children by helping them resolve their trauma and integrate their traumatic experiences into their biography. In crisis intervention, emergency education supports the psychosocial stabilization of children and adolescents; it is first aid for the child soul.

Based on the trauma process outlined earlier, a four-phase model of emergency trauma education emerges:

- **Acute Emergency Education** is introduced in the stages of acute shock with interventions that aim at the physical level.
- **Early Emergency Education** takes place in the phase of posttraumatic stress response with interventions that aim at the level of the life or etheric body.
- **Trauma-oriented special education** is introduced in the phase of posttraumatic disorders and works at the psychosocial level.
- **Trauma-oriented intensive education** is introduced in the phase of chronic PTSD with lasting personality changes following extreme stress. This phase can be seen as the biographical level of intervention.

Emergency education is used during the first two phases of the trauma process (Landolt, 2004, 72), at the time when it becomes apparent whether or not the trauma will take a pathological course. Emergency education aims at activating and strengthening the powers of self-healing in traumatized children in order to enable them to resolve the trauma before posttraumatic stress disorders can develop. "Instant help saves a longer path of suffering" (Morgan, 2007, 11). Emergency education is a part of trauma education.

Waldorf Education as Part of International Crisis Intervention

Since 2006 special needs teachers, physicians, psychologists, and therapists from the Parzival School Center in Karlsruhe (Germany) have, together with volunteers from other anthroposophic professions, been providing emergency education in crisis intervention assignments all over the world. These Emergency Education teams are trying to help traumatized children and adolescents in disaster or war zones. They are deployed by the Friends of Waldorf Education, an aid organization that promotes Waldorf education worldwide.

Emergency education begins in the first weeks that follow a war or natural disaster. Its interventions are based on the principles of Waldorf education and oriented in the traumatological concepts described above, as well as on the special guidelines for dealing with traumatized children and adolescents in a state of acute shock and during the period of early intervention. Emergency education strives to stabilize trauma victims and stimulate their powers of self-healing and coping mechanisms in order to enable them to resolve and overcome their trauma.

Wherever possible, the usually fifteen-strong Emergency Education teams include local teachers and therapists in their work. Apart from the emergency program for traumatized children and youngsters, the team also offers support and information to parents. These parents often suffer because they fail to understand the changed behavior of their traumatized children, who overstep boundaries and break rules, become irritable or aggressive, run away or even hit their parents. Since many of these parents are severely traumatized themselves, they tend to either overreact or give up. Training seminars and courses in

Emergency Education are also offered to local teachers and educators so they can learn to deal with trauma-induced behavioral problems in children and adolescents.

These acute educational emergency interventions are usually followed up by aftercare programs that aim to avoid the break-up of relationships, introduce the necessary measures if children and adolescents have developed pathological posttraumatic stress symptoms, and support the necessary restructuring activities.

Between 2006 and 2011, fifteen Emergency Education interventions with subsequent aftercare operations were carried out in the war and disaster zones described below.

Lebanon 2006: "A Traumatized Country"

> "I was shocked when the missiles began to hit us. I was shaking and lost control over my body. My own weakness affected the children badly. Since that time my five-year-old son vomits after every attack."

This is how a mother describes her ordeal during Israel's air strike on Beirut in 2006. In 2006 and 2007, following the armistice in the Israeli-Lebanese conflict, Emergency Education interventions were carried out in schools and special needs kindergartens in Beirut, Baalbek, and in the Palestinian refugee camp of Shatila (Schiller, 2007a, 2007b).[2]

China 2008: "When Worlds Tumble Down"

> At 2.28 p.m., our school building suddenly jolted and we heard a deep growling noise. We were having our lunch break; the children were sleeping. I didn't realize at first that it was an earthquake. When the tremor got stronger panic broke out. Everybody just ran around. The children cried and screamed. Since the staircase had collapsed all escape routes were blocked. Many children jumped out of the windows. Then the ceiling came down. Amidst all the

---

2. Emergency team Lebanon (2006–2007): Claudia Bartholomeyczik, Myrta Faltin, Georg Kreuer, Barbara Schiller (team leader), Dr. Renate Späth, Timon Tröndle, Sebastian von Tschammer, Erika Wickenhäuser.

*Destroyed temples and shaken soul landscapes
in the earthquake region of Sichuan, China, June 2008*

dust I managed to grasp hold of a girl's hand, but I couldn't get her free. One boy was hanging upside down in the staircase for a day and a half. His legs were trapped. Moments after we managed to free him he died, like many other children who did not survive their rescue. There were maimed bodies everywhere. On the day after the earthquake the second floor collapsed, killing the children who were still trapped. More than 160 children and colleagues died. I cannot remember anything from before the earthquake. I still have no feelings. I am dead even though I am still alive.

Similar tragedies to this one, described by 33-year-old village schoolteacher Xu Xingyou from Hongbai, were experienced by many children, parents, and teachers in the disastrous earthquake in the Chinese province of Sichuan in May 2008. Emergency Education teams went to schools, tent cities and factories in the mountains near Shifang (Ruf, 2008b).[3]

---

3. Emergency team China (2008): Stefanie Allon, Christoph Doll, Dr. Olaf Koob, Bernd Ruf (team leader), Sebastian von Tschammer, Warja Saacke.

Gaza Strip 2009: "The Shooting Continues in the Heads"

After Israeli military strikes in 2009 emergency education interventions were carried out in the Gaza Strip (Ruf, 2009a, 2009b, 2009c).

> Because of their severe injuries many children in the Gaza Strip are unable to leave their flats. Others are so badly traumatized they hide in their flats and have panic attacks when they are asked to leave the house. Others again are hidden or locked away by their despairing parents because of the psychopathological disorders they have developed.
>
> Farrah, who is 2½ years old, lives with the surviving members of her peasant family in the remains of their burned-down house in Northern Gaza. The blood marks in the hallway have been painted over now, but the kitchen is still coal-black. On January 4, 2009, phosphorous shells hit the flat where 16 members of the family had sought shelter (Melzer, 2010, 332ff.). Farrah's grandfather, Sadaka (45), and her brothers Adavahim (14), Zad (12) and Hamsa (9) burned to death. Her sister Shakes (1½) was being nursed by her mother, when the wave of the blast killed her. Six other family members were badly injured. When they were taken to hospital, two cousins of Farrah's who arrived with a cart to help them, were shot dead by soldiers. Farrah and her mother Ghada (20) ended up in a military hospital in Egypt. The crisis team of the Friends of Waldorf Education tried to visit the child there but failed due to bureaucratic hurdles. Farrah's mother died of her injuries. Farrah also has severe phosphor burns. Back in Gaza, she is in a tent hospital, her still "smoking wounds" dressed in a makeshift way with a silicone sheet.
>
> In addition to her physical injuries Farrah has received severe wounds to her soul. Once a cheerful girl, she has not played since the horrific event. She has withdrawn and she suffers from eating and digestive disorders. She is given sleeping pills in the evening so she can fall asleep, but in the night she wakes up screaming, tormented by nightmares and covered in sweat. Farrah is fixated on her father, Mohamed (24). She panics and gets confused when they are separated. Tearfully, her 45-year-old grandmother Sabah Salama Al Suleima Abu Halami says, "Not only are the burns on her body hurting; this child also has no future!"

In Gaza City, Khan Yunis, Zeitoun and Salatin the Emergency Education team worked with hundreds of severely traumatized children and youngsters in tent cities, holiday camps, orphanages, schools and in the actual ruins. Counseling was provided for afflicted families and specialist helpers were trained in seminars. In cooperation with the cultural center, Al Qattan Center for the Child, in Gaza City, follow-up operations have been agreed upon and building work has started on a child protection center in Zeitoun. Specialist training seminars for teachers are being offered and intense support programs are now running in ten preschool institutions. Since 2010 the follow-up operations have been funded by the German Foreign Office.[4]

Indonesia 2009: "Devastated Soul Landscapes"

In November 2009 crisis intervention began in schools and refugee camps in the earthquake-hit area of West Sumatra, Indonesia (Ruf, 2010a). Malalak, a mountain village with 2,227 inhabitants, was devastated by the earthquake and resulting landslides. Sixty-two people died. Of 808 homes, 545 were destroyed; a further 21 were buried beneath the ruins. Many people, including 12 children, had gathered for prayer in the mosque when the earthquake struck. Joru is 30 years old. When the tremors started she was breastfeeding her 14-month-old daughter on the terrace of her little house. Her voice is thin and monotonous: "I saw my 12-year-old son Boy run from the collapsing mosque toward our house. About 3 meters short of our terrace he was carried away and buried by the landslide. We still haven't found him." Boy is one of nine children who are still missing in Malalak.[5]

---

4. Emergency team Gaza Strip (2009–2011): Elisabeth Baumann, Fiona Bay, Heike Böhret, Dr. Pia Büchi, Mirja Cordes, Dr. Peter Elsen, Monika Görzel-Straube, Manfred Hartmann, Diana Jessen, Friedgart Kniebe, Georg Kreuer, Alexa Kuenburg, Peter Lang, Christiaan Liedorp, Lukas Mall, Grit Malsch, Kristina Manz (team leader), Dr. Elke Mascher, Dr. Claudia McKeen, Bernhard Merzenich, Ursula Middelkamp, Yoko Miwa, Marie Pfister, Jenny Rüter, Bernd Ruf (team leader), Bruno Sandkühler, Micaela Sauber, Anni Sauerland, Katrin Sauerland, Hans-Joachim Sennock, Kristian Stähle-Ario, Dimitri Vinogradov, Annekatrin Vogler, Heidi Wolf.

5. Emergency team Indonesia (2009): Vina Bunyamin, Class Kluever, Dr. Matthias Lohn, Lukas Mall, Kristina Manz, Yoko Miwa, Bernd Ruf (team leader), Warja Saacke, Annie Sauerland, Carsten Troll, Carmen Will.

Not even the presidential palace in the Haitian capital of Port-au-Prince withstood the devastating earthquake of January 12, 2010.

Haiti 2010: "Desperate, Disturbed, Deserted"

In January 2010, a devastating earthquake shook Haiti, claiming more than 230,000 human lives. In an orphanage in Santo, a suburb of Port-au-Prince, the Emergency Education team meets Marie-José, the founder of the Hope for Haitian Children Foundation. She runs five homes with more than 200 children. On the campus in Santo we meet 53 of them—orphans, Aids orphans, economic orphans, and street children. Ernson (12) comes hobbling toward us on crutches. He doesn't want to put weight on his injured leg. Nicodem (12) has injuries on his lower left leg and contusions on the left side of the chest. "When the earthquake began, Franky (24), Ernson (12) and I (Nicodem, 12) were on the balcony on the second floor of the home. Franky wanted to save himself by jumping, but he didn't do it because he didn't want to leave us alone. Then the building collapsed on top of us. We were squashed together like one body and couldn't move. Herrig, a 24-year-old student, spoke with us from outside during the many hours we were buried. After more than 12 hours we were dug out and taken to hospital in the school bus. I saw many children with bleeding head injuries. Many died on the way. Franky died in hospital. The doctors thought Ernson and I were dead, too. We were put with the dead bodies. When Ernson and I came round we crept back to the hospital. Every night I dream that I cannot move. I call my brother, Master, who comes and turns me in bed. Then I fall asleep again." While Nicodem can speak fluently about his experience, Ernson can't remember anything. He speaks in a soft voice, his answers are monosyllabic, and he clings tightly to his crutches.

Emergency Education interventions were carried out in the orphanages and slums of Port-au-Prince, in cooperation with the aid organization Our Little Brothers and Sisters. Together with the local organization Acrederp and the German child aid organization Kindernothilfe, it was possible to set up two shelters for over 700 children in Léogâne and to train and employ around 30 native specialists (Ruf, 2010b, c).[6]

Kyrgyzstan 2010: "Pillaged, Displaced, Murdered"

At the request of the Kyrgyz ministry of education Emergency Education was carried out in four schools in Osh in Southern Kyrgyzstan in November 2010, following pogrom-like interethnic conflicts between Kyrgyz and Uzbeks that claimed 2,000 lives.

> "I always got along well with my Kyrgyz neighbors," says Manzura Nargiza (42) from the Cheryomushki district where Kyrgyz and Uzbeks had always lived side by side peacefully: "Now 200 houses have been torched. Next-door to us a family of seven burned to death, including my 76-year-old neighbor, who was holding her grandson in her arms. We live in tents now. There is still shooting going on every night and Uzbek men are hunted down. They want to drive us away so they can build high-rise buildings on our land!" Nadir (18) adds: "I spoke with my boyfriend on the mobile for 15

---

6. Emergency teams Haiti (2010): Christoph Doll, Wibke Falk, Juliana Hepp, Eric Hurner, Julija Kodrevataja, Christiaan Liedorp, Grit Malsch, Lukas Mall, Kristina Manz, Michaela Mezger, Yoko Miwa, Adeline Moelo, Mechthild Pellmann, Dr. Johannes Portner, Bernd Ruf (team leader), Annie Sauerland, Dr. Elke Schmidt, Dr. Michael Schnur, Birgit Marie Stoewer, Dimitri Vinogradov, Heidi Wolf.

Countless arson attacks were among the atrocities committed during the conflicts in Kyrgyzstan in the summer of 2010.

minutes, until he died. Later I found him and his whole family in the cellar of their burned-down house!"

Apart from delivering emergency education to around 1500 pupils, the intervention team offered further training to teachers and trainers in the area and information sessions for parents on trauma symptoms and posttraumatic disorders (Ruf, 2011a).[7]

Japan 2011: "Haunting Images—Haunted Souls"

The triple disaster that hit Northern Japan on March 11, 2011, was particularly challenging for all international crisis intervention

---

7. Emergency team Kyrgyzstan (2010): Monika Görzel-Straube, Christiaan Liedorp, Grit Malsch, Lukas Mall, Kristina Manz, Yoko Miwa, Dr. Ulrike Preisser, Bernd Ruf (team leader), Anna Slavinuk, Dimitri Vinogradov, Heidi Wolf.

teams worldwide. Just a few days after the catastrophe happened, an Emergency Education team was ready and would have flown to Japan if it had not been for the nuclear disaster in Fukushima that followed the earthquake and the tsunami. The meltdown in several reactors and the release of radioactive material on March 12 rendered the situation entirely unpredictable. No one was prepared for the ultimate "maximum credible accident" (MCA). Before any crisis intervention could go ahead, expert risk assessments had to be completed and possible risk scenarios played through in preparation for drawing up an intervention plan and deciding on the necessary equipment. The team members received special training from radiation protection experts of the Karlsruhe Fire Services and the nuclear emergency services (a specialized fire brigade for nuclear incidents in Germany, based in Karlsruhe) to prepare them for their challenging mission. Retreat scenarios for particular situations and locations were worked out in minute detail.

Because of this specialist training the Emergency Education team could only set off on April 27, 2011. In the Japanese disaster area they carried out interventions, advised parents, and trained teachers in the schools and refugee camps around Sendai.[8] Aside from their educational work with around 300 children, 200 teachers, and 120 parents they trained around 70 teachers, educators, physicians, and therapists for further Emergency Education interventions in the crisis area. The intervention team had brought specialist nuclear measuring equipment with them. During their sojourn in Japan the team members were informed daily by the Federal Office for Radiation Protection and the nuclear emergency services in Germany on the most recent developments. Every day, the situation was reassessed on the basis of this information. After returning from the disaster area the members of the emergency team were immediately examined by medical radiation

---

8. Emergency team Japan (2011): Susan Gay, Monika Görzel-Straube, Dr. Bärbel Irion, Grit Malsch, Akiko Matsunaga, Jörg Merzenich, Sibylle Naito, Mechthild Pellmann, Bernd Ruf (team leader), Markus Seitz.

*The Emergency Education team of the Friends of
Waldorf Education in Japan, May 2011*

experts from the Institute for Technology at Karlsruhe University (KIT). Team members and luggage tested negative; no raised levels of radiation were registered. The Emergency Education operation in Northern Japan was funded by the Federal Ministry for Family, Senior Citizens, Women and Youth (Ruf 2011 b).[9]

As a support organization for the psychosocial health of children in war and disaster zones, the Friends of Waldorf Education have

---

9. We received much valuable support during the preparation and follow-up stages as well as during the actual intervention. We would like to thank in particular Dr. Klaus Eiben, chemist; Stefan Prüssmann, head of the Nuclear Aid Services in Eggenstein-Leopoldshafen; Joachim Pech, radiation protection expert with the Karlsruhe Fire Fighters; the Medical Services of the radiation accident department of the Karlsruhe Institute of Technology, the Federal Office for Radiation Protection and not least our Japanese partners, especially Kai Imura and Kimiko Ishikava.

joined the aid organization association Aktion Deutschland Hilft, one of three major German alliances for disaster relief. Waldorf Emergency Education is now part of the international disaster management network.

4

Healing the Frozenness of Trauma

First Aid for the Souls of Japan's Traumatized Children

Safe Places for the Children in Japan's Death Zones

> In a Japanese child aid organization center in Shishogahama local helpers are being trained for an intervention. The organization operates child shelters in Kokusai Nura, Ekiraku, and Mazukase. Head psychologist Takashi Sako (48) is leading an orientation session for educational staff who are going to be working with traumatized children: "Don't reject what the children say, but be open to their signals! Meet the children politely and respectfully! Don't impose anything on them, leave them free!"

THE DAMAGE CAUSED BY EARTHQUAKES is both outer and inner. As the world around collapses, the landscape of the child's soul is destroyed. Rebuilding is required, both internally and externally.

In the aftermath of a catastrophe, children need immediate, competent help. They need to feel safe, outwardly and inwardly, because without this profound sense of safety their wounds will not heal.

The aid organizations in Japan's disaster areas have set up shelters, called Child-Friendly Spaces, where the children's physical, psychosocial, and spiritual needs are catered to. Here, the children can meet and play with educational support from specially trained adults. The skills they acquire here help them deal with the consequences of their harrowing experiences.

The Child-Friendly Spaces in the disaster zones of Northern Japan aim to reach as many children as possible. They are run by local teachers, educators, and social workers and are open to all children, offering safety, a structured environment, and continuity so that the traumatized children can find new trust in themselves, in other people, and in the world around them. They also offer age-appropriate programs to help children resolve their trauma.

Child shelters like those in Kokusai Nura, Ekiraku, and Mazukase also offer the chance to identify children who are injured, sick, disabled, or in need of any other kind of help. The staff in these shelters can tell which of the children are so traumatized that they need immediate medical help or therapy.

Finally, it is crucial that the children who attend the Child-Friendly Spaces are being registered, because that is the only way to identify children who are left without a family or who have been reported missing.

Shelters like the Child-Friendly Spaces can be set up in community centers, emergency tents, or simply in the open air in refugee camps. What is important is that the children feel safe.

Child-Friendly Spaces cater to the needs of children by offering support at various levels, such as space, time, relationships, biography, and speech (Ding, 2009).

Structured Space

> Yoshinori, a thirteen-year-old boy from Shishigahama lost his sense of orientation after his home was buried by the floods. "*Sometimes I don't even know where front and back are, or right and left. I have problems finding my way around big buildings. Even on simple routes that I have walked thousands of times I keep losing my way.*"

Child-Friendly Spaces have a clear spatial structure (**level of space**). They offer activity and rest areas, workshops, eating spaces, and a place for communal activities. Above all, they provide clear and transparent behavior rules. Structured spaces and clear rules provide boundaries, shelter, and safety for children who have lost orientation after a traumatic experience.

*Movement games in the Child-Friendly Space set up
by the Friends of Waldorf Education in Léogâne, Haiti*

Structured Time (Rhythm)

> "I find it very difficult to fall asleep in the evening although I am dead tired. I am so scared of the night. In my dreams I always see my friend Minoru drowning," says Yukio, a 10-year-old boy. Fourteen-year-old Tomoko complains about eating problems: "I saw many people crying for help who were carried away by the floods. But I was unable to help them. The images keep coming back. The awful memories only go away if I eat loads. Then I throw up again." Akira (9) suffers from asthma attacks, Kayoko (5) has diarrhea, Sakae (6) has developed a stammer.

Most traumatized children suffer from rhythmic disorders. Child shelters therefore need to offer clear temporal structures (**level of time**). A structured day with clear rhythms and rituals conveys safety and orientation. There needs to be a time for playing, for artistic activities, for projects, and for exercise. Sports, gymnastics, eurythmy, dancing, and movement games are important strategies for fighting the "monster 'trauma'" (Fietzek, 2006). It is essential that children can express their traumatic experiences verbally. If children can speak about their ordeal it will be easier for them to cope with and resolve their trauma. They must, however, never be forced to speak. Child-Friendly Spaces encourage children to express their trauma in alternative, creative ways. There are all kinds of artistic activities that can help children work through their trauma. Painting, drawing, modeling, drama, and music are activities that allow them to express their stressful experiences and help their inner wounds to heal.

Attachment and Relationships

In extremely stressful situations children need the presence of a calm, mentally stable adult so they are not overwhelmed by existential fears or lose temporal and spatial orientation.

> "When the sea of houses tore away our street I was left all alone. I was terrified and cried for my mother. No-one came to help me," says 12-year-old Sumichi from Osato.

When disasters happen children are often left alone, helpless, and without protection. The trauma severs their connection with their own body, the world, and other people. Fostering attachment and relationships is therefore a crucial pedagogical task. Reliable relationships need building up again. **Relationships** are seen as another priority (aside from spatial and temporal structures) in child shelters when a major disaster has happened. "The personality of the educator is of central importance in trauma education" (Kühn, 2009, 33). Neurobiology emphasizes the healing influence of pedagogical role models in child development and in the mitigation of traumatic experiences (Bauer, 2006, 117ff.). Traumatized children in particular need adult role models who provide them with healing images and experiences (Besser, 2009, 51; Hüther, 2008).

Daily rhythm and rituals provide safety, support, and orientation

Correcting Traumatic Experiences

"When the world tumbled down around me I couldn't do anything. I was unable to help myself or anybody else. I couldn't run away. I was like pinned to the ground. I just couldn't do anything. Since then I haven't felt anything and I'm scared of every new day," says Suishi (12) who lost his brothers and sisters in the floods.

Traumatized children and youngsters have experienced the inconceivable. Child shelters must therefore be places where, consistently, new positive experiences can be made that can gradually mitigate the trauma (biographical level).

Through trauma children are caught in a past that seems impossible to overcome. They lose all hope of a future they can actively shape. Often, they withdraw after their experience of powerlessness. There is a danger of all activity coming to a halt, a situation that would

A healthy teacher-child relationship creates trust and stability.

aggravate the effect of the trauma. These experiences of helplessness can be mitigated by planning and carrying out age-appropriate projects with the children.

Arts and crafts, ecological, or charitable projects can unblock the victims' creative potential and allow them to become actively involved again. The children begin to trust again that they can have an effect on the world and that they can take hold of their own life.

Small- or larger-scale building projects can be very effective. Trauma means that the soul is wounded. The organism's protective mantle has been injured and new skin needs to grow. According to psychologists, children's drawings of houses are self-projections. A child's body is his or her house. Under normal circumstances the house offers safety and protection to the child soul; it is a "safe place." Trauma means that this safe place breaks down; the protective mantle is torn. Children lose all sense of protection, safety, or comfort. Building tree houses, yurts, tepees, or simple caves made from fabric can help create new protective layers.

The children's negative experiences of helplessness can be replaced when they have the possibility of experiencing themselves as competent and as being able to realize their intentions. Experiencing self-efficacy is healing!

> Since the earthquake Masataka (15) was hardly able to remember anything. The only memories that remained were those of the destruction: "Important parts of my life are missing from my memory. I keep coming up against black holes when I try to remember. I'm often unable to tell whether something happened earlier or later in my life. The order of events has become muddled."

Trauma can block memories and temporal orientation. When this happens it can help to work with young people on their "lifeline" by using a rope. The beginning of the rope represents the time of their birth, where the rope ends is the present moment. The adolescents walk along this rope that symbolizes their "life line." Happy events are marked with flowers or blossoms, painful experiences with stones. This kind of biography work can help to restructure the victims' memory and bring new order to their experience of time.

The community can also be a healing influence (Perry and Szalavitz, 2009, 291ff.). Pedagogical group work and socialization processes can help break down the power trauma has over its victim and prevent further negative impressions.

Neurobiology is finding evidence for the concept of mitigating trauma in the "brain's experiential plasticity" (Bauer, 2009, 71). Neuronal networks in the brain grow stronger with use while unused synapses tend to regress and disappear. "Use it or lose it!" is the neurobiological maxim. "Synapses that are used often are strengthened, while ones that aren't used often are weakened and might be lost altogether" (Ibid., 59). Traumatic experiences can be corrected!

Fostering Speech

The **level of speech** also needs catering for in the aftermath of trauma. Children who are in shock frequently cannot comprehend complex sentences or multiple simultaneous instructions. It is important that we speak clearly and slowly with them, that we repeat and use simple, short sentences.

Speech can be therapeutic after extreme trauma if its use is not restricted to communicating or the passing on of information. Artistic speech or speech therapy exercises can reduce and resolve stress-induced speech blockages.

Sounds are not mechanical utterances but have evolved in a formative process. While vowels express inner experiences, feelings, emotions, and sensations, consonants have evolved as the result of external configurative forces. "In speaking vowels we take hold of ourselves and the space around us from the inside. Consonants form us from the outside" (Vogel, 2007, 171). While each sound has an essential basic gesture, it can also have various nuances; the open "Ah" sound that expresses wonder has a different soul quality from the "A" at the beginning of the word "ask" and will be expressed differently in eurythmy. "Each sound has an archetypal gesture but this gesture must be differentiated depending on what comes to expression" (Bardt, 2010, 19).

As early as 1924, Rudolf Steiner described how, when we speak, we generate movement in the air in front of our mouths. We have technical means today of making this movement visible. "When we form a word we press out the air in a certain gesture. Someone who has suprasensory vision and can see the forms that stream out of the mouth, perceives specific gestures in the air; they are the words" (Steiner, 1982, CW 276, 130; cf. also Steiner, 1968, CW 279, 47). In experiments with high-speed photography carried out over years, Johanna Zinke was able to prove and document this process (Zinke, 2003). Every sound creates a characteristic, reproducible air movement in front of the speaker's mouth. These forms sometimes linger for seconds after the

*Speech and movement exercises can harmonize
trauma-induced rhythmic disorders.*

sound waves have subsided. "Every sound produces a streaming form. To begin with, speech is therefore a form-creating movement process" (Patzlaff, 1999, 791). In synchrony with the emerging air-sound-forms, all muscles in the speaker's body perform subtle, invisible movement patterns with every sound that is spoken. These movements can also be captured by a high-speed camera (Lutzker, 1996, 38ff.). Kinesiology researcher William S. Condon found out "that when we listen to speech sounds we imitate, from top to toe, the same subtle movements that the speaker is carrying out unconsciously. This imitation is almost simultaneous. The delay of 40 to 50 milliseconds is so small that a conscious response is out of the question" (Patzlaff, 1999, 792). There is no connection between the two processes that could be physically explained. It is "as if speaker and listener shared a medium of rhythmic movement" (ibid., 792). This is true for all languages.

Condon observed that two-year-old babies respond to various languages with the corresponding subtle body movements (Condon and Sander, 1974). "It is as if the body of the listener was dancing in precise and fluid accompaniment to the spoken word" (Condon, quoted in Lutzker, 1996, 43).

Trauma massively disrupts the formative rhythmic movement processes of sound formation and the rhythmic interaction between speaker and listener. Speech and movement can have a harmonizing influence on trauma-induced speech disorders. Artistic speech exercises and eurythmy as "visible speech" or "visible song" (Siegloch and Maier-Smits, 1993) have proved to be particularly effective remedies in such cases.

> Yutaka (12) who lost both his parents in the tsunami is sitting in a corner of his six-square-meter cardboard box in the gym hall of Onagawa, which has been turned into a refugee camp. He has not spoken a word since the disaster happened.

Extreme trauma can leave children unable to speak. It is very common for children and youngsters to develop speech or speaking disorders after trauma (Dohm, 2002, 14ff.) because the shock causes tensions in the motor functions of respiration and speech that lead to speech blocks.

Many children develop a stammer when they are in shock. "The pressure of breath in the mouth and on the lips is increased. For the lips to open both tensions must be in agreement. When the lips become tense and don't open elastically the speaker develops a stutter" (Baur, 1995, 126). Stutters can manifest at three levels; when we connect sounds, when we connect words with thoughts, and when we connect with other people (ibid., 130). These speech-specific "*attachment problems*" can be accompanied by diverse rhythmic disorders; the breathing rhythm is as disrupted as is the rhythm of the human interaction. This happens due to the existential fears elicited after we have lost all trust and sense of safety. A stutter is the organic manifestation of fear. Because fear puts children under pressure, they breathe in tensely, but their breathing out is congested, causing their breath to stop. The soul and feeling life grow tense within the physical organization. Children who stutter have often been prevented by blockages from realizing their life intentions. "A stutter is not strictly speaking a speech impediment; it is destiny manifesting in the speech process.... It is therefore very important that we don't just aimlessly treat the symptoms.... We need to find out where and when the congestion occurs" (ibid., 135). The speaking of anapest verse (short-short-long) has been shown to relieve blockages and congestions in the breathing process, while slurred consonants respond well to the structuring influence of the dactyl (long-short-short) (Steiner and Steiner-von Sievers, 1981, CW 282, September 7, 1924).

Playing with sounds, words, speech rhythms, verses, and rhymes can help children overcome speech disorders, especially if the sounds are accompanied by gestures and movement. Speech exercises are an important part of trauma work in emergency education.

Help for Parents

> "Ever since the tsunami happened my 16-year-old son Taro has come into our bed, night after night, bathed in sweat and filled with terror. I don't know what to do," says Aiken (45). "I am glad I can come here for advice!"

Child shelters that are run as Child Friendly Spaces also offer advice to parents. Parents often struggle to understand the behavioral changes in their children following a disaster. It is important to explain the nature of trauma to parents—how it can manifest and what their children's activities can hope to achieve. It is helpful to set up centers adjacent to Child-Friendly Spaces where parents can meet, share their experiences, and help each other.

> In the child shelter Mazukase in Shishigahama the children are sitting under a colorful parachute. Before they sat down, they had been standing in a circle, balancing a ball on the parachute. This

activity requires a high degree of concentration, orchestrated movements and, above all, cooperation. It is a pedagogical exercise that enhances the ability for teamwork that, along with all other social skills, has been severely disrupted by the trauma. When the exercise is finished the mood is so relaxed, that the emergency teacher feels encouraged to ask if someone has a question. Gradually, one after the other, the children begin to speak. Nine-year-old Tetsunari tells an abstruse story that plays in a world consisting of feces. The story of Fukui (10) who sits next to him is set in a chaotic underwater world. Hideyoshi (11) describes a world where the sun no longer wants to shine.

The stories are informed by sadness and hopelessness. But slowly, the children begin to open up. They tell their stories in pictures. This opening up can only happen in the protected space of a safe relationship, in a place where the children feel safe. The parachute they sit under can become such a place of safety.

"My friend no longer needs the bike. He's dead."

Lessons at Ookawa primary school in Ishinomaki had just finished when the earth trembled, and destruction struck the North of Japan on an apocalyptic scale. Around 40 of the children had already been picked up by their parents. Three teachers were off work. In keeping with the school's tsunami crisis plan, the remaining 70 pupils gathered with their eleven teachers at the designated collection point. However, the place that was meant to provide safety turned out to be a death trap. All the children and teachers were carried off by the tsunami and drowned. Only one teacher and three children, who had gone against the instructions and fled up a mountain, survived. Ookawa primary school in Ishinimaki has become the national symbol of Japan's black day.

The survivors are not happy about their escape. They are apathetic and feel empty inside. Many of them harbor feelings of guilt. Teachers who survived are depressed and suicidal. Many parents blame themselves for not picking up their children from school that day; others simply feel ashamed because they are still alive.

Tsuyoshi (7) is a pupil at Ookawa primary school in Ishinomaki. He lost his three cousins, all of his classmates and his neighbors in

Healing the Frozenness of Trauma

Form drawing supports trauma resolution in Japan, May 2011.

the tsunami. He survived because his mother collected him from school. They live with relatives now in Fukuchiaza Kamosaki, a nearby village, where traumatized children and adolescents receive care at the RQ Shimin Sargai Kyuen Center Kohoku.

Since the disaster Tsuyoshi can always be found riding his bike. "It's my friend's bike. He no longer needs it. He's dead." These are the first words Tsuyoshi says when we meet. To begin with he refuses to take part in the emergency education activities. But soon we see him riding his bike on the inward and outward curling spiral, deeply engaged in form drawing exercises or keenly joining in ball games.

This drawing of a Japanese child shows a person drifting in the floods, May 2011.

The other children and youngsters at the center don't display any conspicuous behavior at first, although each of them has experienced high levels of stress. They have lost parents, siblings, friends, and neighbors, their houses were destroyed, their sense of safety is gone. Only gradually they reveal what is concealed behind the façade of pretended normality; they hardly sleep, often cry, suffer from headaches and stomach aches, are haunted by fears and avoid anything that might remind them of the disaster (Karutz and Lagossa, 2008).

To overcome trauma, victims need to speak about their experiences or **express** them in other ways. "Express" literally means "pushing out" experiences, feelings, or thoughts and placing them at a distance. Verbally expressing trauma is part of resolving and integrating the experience. And while victims, especially children, often find it impossible to speak about their traumatic experiences, they can express their feelings, thoughts, memories, fears, and worries in writing. Keeping a diary and writing poems or stories are useful measures toward overcoming trauma.

Young members of the Samouni family, absorbed in flute playing by an Emergency Education team member, Gaza, July 2009

When children draw they bring their experiences to paper. Children's **drawings** are like diary entries that tell stories.

Members of Human Rights Watch gave crayons and paper to child refugees in the border regions between Sudan and Chad to keep them occupied. The children did not need encouragement; they willingly drew their war experiences. Five hundred war documents were created in Darfur by children between the ages of six and eight.[1] The Court in The Hague recognized these shocking images as evidence of human rights violations.

The well-known drawings of 12-year-old Helga Weissova document life in captivity. Helga was taken with her parents to the Theresienstadt concentration camp in December 1941 (Schuster, 1994; Breiter and

---
1. Human Rights Watch (2007). Children's drawings from Darfur: tanks, airplanes, bombs. http://spiegel.de/fotostrecke/0,5538,23641,00.html; October 13, 2007.

Klattenhoff, 2005). Around 100 of her drawings have survived, depicting the oppression and hopelessness experienced by the child.

The children in North Japan's disaster zone draw and paint mainly underwater images that show debris, corpses, and menacing sharks.

The drawings of children give insight into their outer and inner world and reflect their needs and distress. Drawing allows children to express non-verbally what they are unable to put into words and can help them come to terms with their trauma.

Emotional blockages in children can also be resolved through singing and playing music. The musical activity helps them to uncover their buried feelings. Watercolor painting is particularly suitable for healing frozenness and for transforming trauma. Clay modeling helps children experience their own efficacy and overcome the feeling of powerlessness instilled by the trauma.

Drama is another way of expressing trauma without speaking about it directly. The protection of an assumed part can help trauma victims to express their own thoughts and feelings without fear. Also, play-acting involves action and physical movement. It can help overcome feelings of helplessness and dissolve the inner frozenness of trauma. Drama games, role-playing, and puppet shows can do much toward resolving inner struggles and they allow trauma victims to experience their own efficacy again. All forms of creative therapy offer alternative ways of expressing the inconceivable. Creative therapies help resolve the trauma. Art is healing (Eckhardt, 2005)!

MANY CHILDREN ARE AFRAID TO GO TO THE TOILET BY THEMSELVES

> Eisaku Watanabe (29), a teacher from Onagawa, describes the changes he observed in his pupils after the disaster. "Many pupils can't concentrate or lack motivation. They can't function anymore. Hardly any of them want to learn and, what is worse, they refuse to stick to any rules. Most pupils are edgy and frightened. We teachers register a high incidence of illnesses such as infections, allergies, asthma, nausea, headaches, eating and sleeping disorders!"

Healing the Frozenness of Trauma

The 160 primary school students in Onagawa have been through horrific ordeals. From their classrooms they watched how the tsunami tore away and destroyed 90 percent of their town. Fifty-eight parents lost their lives, five children were fully orphaned. In Onagawa the devastation reached apocalyptic dimensions. The water rose up to the school, which stood on a hill. Children and teachers were trapped for three days and nights without food and electricity before the rescue workers finally arrived. Today, parts of the school have been transformed into an emergency center. Many classrooms are used for crisis meetings, as intervention planning venues or for the storing of goods. A multistory refugee camp for thousands of people has been set up in the gym hall. Children and the elderly in particular suffer from trauma-typical infections. The extreme stress has weakened their immune systems, leaving them susceptible to illness. Most of the pupils and teachers at Onogawa primary school live in the refugee camp.

Hanei (25), who teaches class 2, says that many children have grown calmer and more balanced. "But many still wet their beds at night, can't sleep, or suffer from nightmares and massive fears. The frequent aftershocks make the children panic, especially when they are alone on their way to school. Some children refuse to leave their homes. They cling to their mothers. At school they don't dare to go to the toilet by themselves. A teacher needs to go with them!"

Trauma victims become dysfunctional. Children and young people often display severe rhythmic disorders. All rhythms—waking and sleeping, eating, respiration, and digestion, also those of remembering and forgetting, movement, and perception—are out of sync. As a result the victims develop sleeping disorders, attention deficit disorder, eating and digestive disorders, amnesia or flashbacks, breathing and movement disorders, and so on.

Rhythm can be fostered by giving the day a clear rhythmical structure, by doing rhythmic clapping and movement exercises and playing rhythmic ball games. The disrupted biorhythm becomes re-adjusted and the trauma symptoms abate. Rhythm means security, stability, and orientation (Krüger, 2007a). "Repetition, if consciously applied, strengthens the will and motivates children to take action" (Goebel and Glöckler, 2005, 224).

"Finding emotional as well as physical stability is important for trauma sufferers.... Giving structure to the day brings back a degree of stability" (Morgan, 2007, 68). Together with the teachers in Onagawa, the crisis intervention team of the Friends of Waldorf Education has established a rhythmic and structured life at the primary school. At morning assembly the members of the school community speak a verse, practice a round, do rhythmic movement exercises, and walk along inward and outward curling spirals. The assembly is followed by workshops in eurythmy, painting, form drawing, adventure education, and role-play. The gathering at the end of the school day exactly mirrors the morning assembly. "In the early stages, reliable daily rituals help establish a new structure" (Ibid., 36).

The 25 children of class 6 are standing in a circle in their classroom. They are doing eurythmy; first they carry out the gestures for the vowels "I" [ee]—"A" [ah]—"O" [oh] and then they walk in a line in a figure eight. The crossing over in the middle is particularly difficult for trauma victims (this also becomes apparent in form drawing exercises).

Trauma may disrupt the connection between the two brain hemispheres and this has a negative effect on an individual's general well-being. "With rhythmical exercises and crossing-over exercises which enhance brain coordination and functioning we can promote the reconnection between the two sides of the brain. Musical rhythm exercises are particularly suited ..., as are dancing, walking while crossing limbs (for instance, touching the left knee with the right hand and vice versa), eye exercises (eyes wander from a point in the left to one in the right visual field)" (Eckardt, 2005, 68f.).

Traumatized children are usually not well incarnated. Rudolf Steiner described eurythmy as "gymnastics for the soul" (Bardt, 2010, 113). Eurythmy is ensouled movement. It strengthens the connection between body and soul that has become loosened during the traumatic event and is therefore particularly suited to help overcome trauma.

When we speak we also carry out formative, rhythmic movement processes which can be disturbed by trauma. "When we form a word we press out the air in a certain gesture. Someone who has suprasensory

*Eurythmy with rods resolves inner blockages
in Southern Kyrgyzstan, November 2010.*

vision and can see the forms that stream out of the mouth, perceives specific gestures in the air; they are the words. When we imitate these forms, we do eurythmy. Eurythmy is visible expressive gesture just as the forms in the air that appear when we speak are invisible gestures into which our thought enters, creating waves that then become audible. Eurythmy expresses the air gestures as visible gestures of the limb" (Steiner, 1982, CW 276, 130).

Eurythmy as "visible speech" and "expressive gesture" can help melt the frozenness and release the spasms and blockages of trauma, so that the child's spirit-soul can enter into and fully take hold of the body again.

The **circular forms** used in eurythmy, ring games, and dance have a harmonizing effect on individual children as well as on groups of children. Circular forms can enhance the self-experience that was weakened by the trauma. With the growing self-experience the children's self-esteem and self-confidence also grow. "When we feel a circle—in the plane or in space—we feel our "I." You need to know that, as living, sense-perceptive beings we feel how a sense of self arises in our souls when we see a circle, or even only a part of a circle. Seeing a section of a round bowl, for instance, stimulates a sense of autonomy in us" (Steiner, 1982, CW 286, 76).

This explains the appearance of circular forms in the drawings of three-year-olds: "The drawing skills of infants develop in relation to their psychological development. The first undifferentiated scribbles gradually assume a closed, rounded shape.... The circle symbolizes the whole person" (Oppikofer, 2007, 55). When young children draw their first circles they usually also begin to refer to themselves as "I."

Circular forms promote I-awareness and the experience of self and autonomy which are all located at a level of consciousness that can be severely damaged by trauma.

We tend to notice the effectiveness of emergency education beginning on the second day. This was also the case in Onogawa. The behavior of the children changes, their life forces are visibly reactivated, and one can see how they regain joy in life. Rhythms and rituals are healing forces (Eckhardt, 2005)!

Disabilities Become More Pronounced

Most children with developmental disorders have experienced some kind of trauma in early childhood—life-threatening complications during birth, extended hospitalization, medical interventions, or maybe the parents had problems coming to terms with their child's disability. Physical or psychological neglect and abuse are equally common when parents can't cope.

Developmental complications make it difficult for the child's spiritual essence, or "I," to take hold of the deficient body and to exert its regulating and integrating functions. Children with weakened "I"-awareness are in danger of being continuously overwhelmed by excessive sensory stimuli. In children who have what is commonly called intellectual disabilities the "I"-experience tends to be considerably weakened and, as a consequence, these children have a low self-image, low self-trust and a diminished sense of self-worth. Over and above that, these children are often unable to realize their life goals and therefore unable to experience self-efficacy.

As a result "intellectually disabled" children are physically and emotionally less stress-resistant. Between 30 and 50 percent of these children suffer from secondary mental disorders (de Raaf, 2011, 162). They often hardly understand what is going on around them. Because they are unable to reflect sufficiently on their experience of stress or their problems, they are also unable to verbalize them adequately and assimilate them. This leaves them prone to experiences of crisis and stress. Their whole life situation seems to be one big risk factor for trauma.

Japan's black day affected many disabled children. The specific needs of these children tend not to be sufficiently considered when a disaster like the one in Japan happens. **Rifu** has a special needs day center—*Sazan-zi* (Happy House)—that offers support to disabled children and adolescents from the Japanese disaster zone. Around 25 children live here in refugee camps and attend special schools or integrative classes. After losing its building in the disaster, the special needs day center in Tagajo found a new home in two small rooms of a small industrial enterprise.

> Tsie is nine years old. She is rather small for her age; her mouth is open so her large tongue is visible. She has short limbs, her hands have single transverse palm creases and the small fingers are bent,

her eyes characteristically double-lidded; Tsie is a Down syndrome child. Her mother, to whom she was very attached, was carried off by the tsunami. Since the disaster, all Tsie ever wants to do is sit on her caregiver's back in the way Japanese babies are carried by their mothers. Special needs teacher Yuka (43) says, "Since the disaster many children have regressed to developmental stages they had long grown out of. They are fearful and clingy. Their individual disabilities become more pronounced. Some children are hyperactive and aggressive; others are apathetic and withdraw socially. They seem inwardly frozen."

Mentally disabled children are often traumatized by large-scale disasters like the one in Northern Japan. Because of their cognitive restrictions, sudden changes in the conditions around them seem particularly threatening and frightening. If there is no emotionally stable adult around them to calm and reassure them when the disaster happens, traumatization is inevitable. "All highly organized forms of coping require the ability to realize and understand what is happening, to process experiences and to adapt behaviors according to the situation. The more disabled a child is the less developed are these cognitive abilities and the greater the probability that trauma occurs" (Senckel, 2007, 51). Scientific studies (Jantzen, 2003) show "that the vulnerability grows in inverse proportion to a child's intelligence" (Kühn, 2009, 28).

The effect the trauma has on disabled children is not that different from the effect it has on children generally. Disabled children and youngsters also display the trauma-specific symptoms. "It is important, however, that we don't orient ourselves on the child's real age but consider the psychological deviation which, in turn, depends on the degree of disability. The more severe the mental disability the more the symptoms will resemble, both now and when the child will be older, those of traumatized children or even babies" (Senckel, 2007, 54).

> Ayame (14) is sitting in a corner, playing by herself. She does not understand other children's feelings, wishes or thoughts. She tends to be preoccupied with switches. Her playing seems monotonous

> and consists of endless stereotypes. Ayame has an autism spectrum disorder. Since the tsunami she seems even more isolated, withdrawn, and strange. She tries to cope with, or free herself from, her extreme fear of anything unfamiliar by adopting compulsive behavior patterns or giving way to aggressive outbursts. Recently, Ayame has also developed an eating disorder. She only eats rice pudding. Her muscles are tense and hard as rock. Ayame's caregiver, Hisamo (52), says, "She seems to me like hardened lava."

Trauma entails being frozen with shock. Many traumatized children are tense, rigid and frozen in body and soul. According to a Japanese saying, *"the shock sits in the limbs."* This freezing of etheric and emotional energies can lead to developmental retardation and learning difficulties. Trauma-induced blockages therefore need to be released before the symptoms become chronic (Levine and Kline, 2010).

> Apathetically, Fuimo (6) is crouching in another corner of the room. The Head of the day center, Jodi (58), explains, "He used to be a cheerful, outgoing child who loved to play and was full of creative ideas. Since the massive earthquake of 11 March he has not played at all." Fuimo's friend Suishi (5) has not forgotten how to play but his play has changed. He will invariably build landscapes out of wooden bricks that are then carried away by a tsunami. His play is like a never-ending flashback. Psychologists refer to the phenomenon as "traumatic playing."

As a rule children's play tends to be creative and progressive. Children assimilate their experiences through play. Trauma undermines a child's natural play drive. Some children stop playing altogether while others relive their horrific experiences compulsively and unremittingly in their "traumatic play." Traumatic playing is not creative or progressive. It is like a flashback. Traumatized children feel compelled to "reproduce" their trauma in playing. The trauma cannot be assimilated because it keeps recurring.

After a disaster, traumatized children need an adult companion who encourages them to play while gently leading them out of the traumatic play situation.

Kei (9) suffers from rescue syndrome. He witnessed his uncle being carried off by the tsunami. Since then he has only been drawing people without limbs. "His soul has withdrawn from his body. His hands are like empty gloves," says Yodi thoughtfully. Modeling with beeswax can help Kei to take hold of his limbs again.

In an intervention in the Gaza Strip in 2009, the emergency education team helped a woman who was in shock and severely dissociated, to find her center again by encouraging her to model with beeswax. At first the woman kept having aggressive outbursts, tearing the wax into shreds and swearing. But after around twenty minutes she managed to form the wax into a ball. As soon as the rounded shape appeared she was centered again; she responded when she was spoken to and began to speak about her trauma. *"Often the hands can solve a riddle that the intellect has struggled with in vain"* (Jung, 1967).

Circles and spheres have played important educational roles in all cultures (Bardt, 2012, 129). They appear in folktales (gold and crystal balls), as seasonal symbols (Christmas baubles), in games and dances (circle games and dances) or as toys (balls, rings, snowballs, glass beads, marbles, soap bubbles, etc.). "The sphere represents the trinity, with the father god as the center, the son as the circumference and the Holy Spirit as the radius" (Johannes Kepler, as quoted by Steiner, 1980, CW 148, 185). Many of the movements we carry out are based on the sphere or its shadow, the circle—for instance, when we swing our arms when walking. Circular movements often seem accidental but they are not (Bardt, 2010, 129). They are in fact initiated by psychomotor activity. "We can feel our self or I in the form of the circle, when we proceed beyond the purely mathematical knowledge to the actual experience of its form. To experience a circle in the plane or a sphere in space means to experience our self, our 'I'" (Steiner, 1982, CW 286, 76). We therefore employ wood or copper balls for rhythmic circle exercises in emergency education. By using the balls, traumatized children can find their center again and harmoniously experience their own selves.

Healing the Frozenness of Trauma

Eurythmy with balls in the war rubble in Gaza, July 2009, to support centering and a harmonised "I"-experience of traumatised children

Kazuo (12), Ayame's younger brother, is lying on a bench in *Satzan-zi*. He is complaining about a stomachache. Gentle stroking can work wonders with stress-induced stomachaches. Just as in sports, the massaging movements can release cramps.

After the earthquake in China in 2008 one of the trauma victims, a factory worker from Shifang, did not speak for seven weeks. It took only two minutes of gently massaging her upper arms until the woman showed a strong reaction; she was sick and then found her voice again. The frozenness in her limbs, which had been caused by the shock, was released by the massage. The woman's speech returned as soon as she had, in the almost symbolic act of vomiting, freed herself from something she was unable to digest. Especially with traumatized babies and infants, the gentle application of **physical touch** can alleviate stress and release frozen energies.

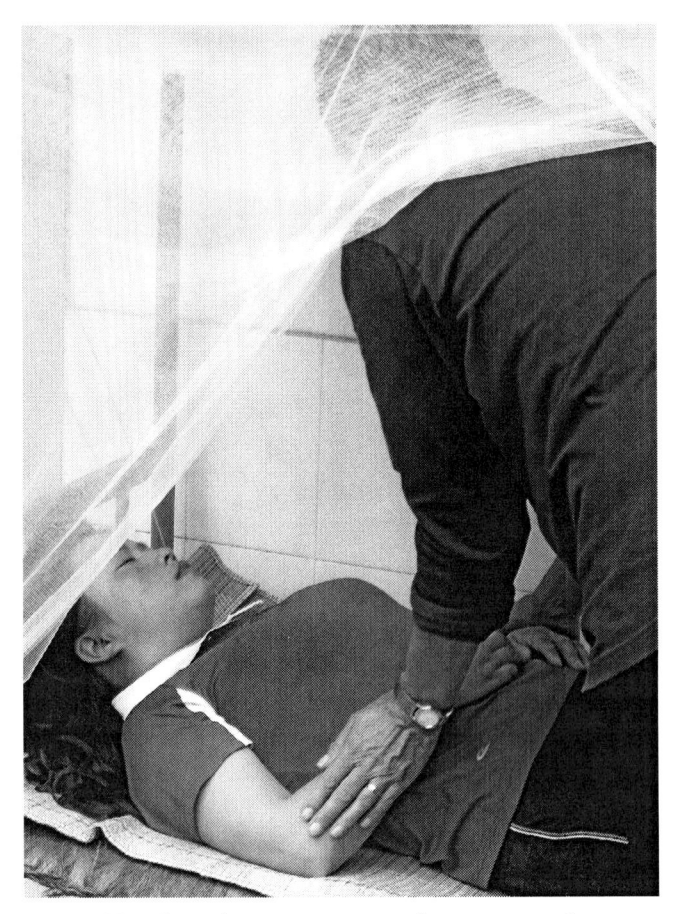

*Touch and massage to resolve a woman's
"frozen" inner being, China, June 2008*

Herbal **compresses or poultices** can also induce deep relaxation and release frozen or blocked energies. **Baths** are relaxing, too. The rhythmic movement of the water eases cramps and blockages and reduces compulsive tendencies. Rhythmic *Einreibungen* also counteracts immobility and frozenness. The etheric oils used in the process create a protective extra skin for hyper-alert, hypersensitive and hyperactive children. These children, who received severe injuries to their souls, can begin to feel at home again in their skin. Most traumatized children need physical contact. It goes without saying

Exercises for training body awareness;
Japanese parents in the earthquake region, May 2011

that any touching requires the child's agreement and must never be forced on a child.

> The children in the special-needs day center *Satzan-zi* are sitting in a circle. The caregivers use their fingers to draw forms or letters on the children's backs.

Trauma disturbs a person's body-awareness and upsets all the basic senses. Some trauma victims are unable to touch the tip of their nose with a finger or find their earlobe. The special needs children in Rifu were helped in a playful way to regain **body awareness**.

Trauma also disrupts children's sensory development. The basic bodily senses (of touch, life, proprioception, and balance), which develop during the first years of life, are profoundly affected and, as a result, the children develop emotional, social-behavioral or

Promoting a feeling for the basic senses in children by kneading; the earthquake region of western Sumatra, Indonesia, November 2009

general behavioral disorders (König 1986, Köhler, 1994). Fostering the senses systematically is therefore a priority in the aftermath of traumatic experiences.

Clay **modeling, kneading** dough for baking, playing with water or sand, modeling with beeswax or papier-mâché and applying **physical touch** through stroking, rubbing, massaging, or applying rhythmic *Einreibungen* are ideal ways of nurturing the sense of touch. The sense of life is best supported through **warmth, rhythm,** and a **balanced and healthy diet.**

Circus games and circus arts, such as acrobatics, stimulate the senses of movement and balance (Lang, 2010, 174ff.). Juggling with balls or veils, walking on stilts, balancing on beams, large balls, or ropes, swinging, skipping, or cycling are activities that generally strengthen the senses of traumatized children.

Healing the Frozenness of Trauma

*Artistic games for children traumatized
by the earthquake in Haiti, May 2010*

Trauma also affects the movement of children or adolescents and can result in rhythmic disorders. Affected children may either grow hyperactive with uncoordinated, sudden urges to move, or become frozen and rigid and resist any movement; "Movement blockages are a sign that the flow of emotions is disturbed" (Hagemann, 2009, 59).

Movement and exercise are therefore key activities in emergency education. Any kind of movement will help dissolve inner blockages, which is why the children and adolescents at the Happy House in Rifu are offered a rich movement program.

Our bodily movements are interrelated with our breathing and heart rhythms.

> Rhythms, those of circulation and respiration in particular, have a direct connection with the rhythms of movement. Walking, running, dancing, but also many work- or sports-related movements have similar temporal forms. Studies have revealed that,

when we walk or run, the ratio between our pace and our pulse often settles in at 1 to 1, which means that there are times when pulse and step coincide. This kind of congruence is particularly noticeable in children.... We walk in the rhythm of our pulse! (Rosslenbroich, 1994, 132).

Studies in chronobiology investigating body rhythms during movement have shown "that we each have our own rhythm of pulse, breathing and movement and that we unconsciously try to attune these rhythms to each other" (Ibid., 132f.). Findings from sports medicine research corroborate these results. With top athletes there is an obvious "phase synchronization between movement and heart rate as they tend to place their steps during the heart's systole" (Ibid., 133).

Rhythmic movements generally tend to be experienced as pleasant. We can soothe traumatized babies by rocking or carrying them rhythmically. Rocking horses and garden swings can help young children overcome trauma-induced movement disorders. "Rhythmic movements enhance the maturation of the rhythmic organization" (Rosslenbroich, 1994, 133).

Even a simple walk can stimulate the healing process. Trauma disrupts the coordination between the two halves of the brain. The mere rhythm of walking can have a profound and lasting beneficial effect on the synchronization between the brain hemispheres.

Exercises with skipping ropes can support trauma work. The swinging rope can symbolize a threat that, once tackled, is like the experience of a successful escape. Skipping helps alleviate fears. Children who are too afraid of the rope can achieve a similar sense of success by "pretend skipping" without a rope (Levine and Kline, 2008, 210). This exercise also stimulates the child's imagination in preparation for potential imaginative intervention techniques.

Movement games in the group enhance child resilience. Physical activity can release energies that have become frozen in a dangerous situation. Many group games are based on the flight-or-fight response and allow children to release blocked energies. It is, however, equally

*Dance games to help integrate energy,
southern Kyrgyzstan, November 2010*

important to schedule in resting times for the children because excess energies can be discharged in the **activity as well as in the resting phase.**

Circle games with sudden changes of direction are particularly suitable for building up and discharging etheric or emotional energies. They nurture the child's biological rhythms and promote healing. Eurythmy, eurythmy therapy, and form drawing involve changes of direction that strengthen the life or ether body (Vogel, 2007, 88).

Ring games and circle or folk dances reflect cosmic-planetary movements and the procession of the sun through the zodiac. We use these games and dances in emergency education to strengthen and stabilize children and young people after traumatic events. Circular forms convey inner calm, harmony, and confidence. They represent the order of human, social, and cosmic relationships that has been damaged by the trauma. Apart from enhancing our experience of self and "I"-awareness circular forms also support community building.

The circle form as such creates community. Circular forms counteract the trauma victim's tendency to withdraw and become isolated. The circle offers protection and can become a "safe place."

Ring and circle games and folk dances are particularly suited to reestablish a sense of safety, harmony, calm, community, and order. Movement heals (Eckhardt, 2005)!

How String Games Help Resolve Trauma

The Tohoku Museum in Tagajo, a monumental concrete building, was severely damaged in the earthquake. One hundred twenty children from Waldorf kindergartens with their parents and educators have gathered here. They walk in a circle, singing. The circle opens into a spiral, winding first inward, then outward. Nine-year-old Mieko is standing away from the group, shivering, pale. Her face is without expression, frozen; her gaze is empty. "Since the earthquake she hasn't taken part in anything. She is withdrawn, fearful, and highly vulnerable. She never sleeps through the night because she dreams that the end of the world has come. Now she has developed asthma and indigestion on top of everything else," says her mother Yukie (34).

Trauma disrupts most biological rhythms and this can result in speech disorders (stutter), breathing problems (asthma), and sleep disorders (problems falling and staying asleep).

The newborn baby begins life by breathing in for the first time (incarnation) and our life ends at the moment of death when we breathe out for the last time (excarnation). Breathing-in makes us more conscious, because, when we inhale, our spirit-soul can enter our physical and life body more deeply, whereas it becomes more detached from them when we breathe out. The rhythm of waking and sleeping is also one of contracting and expanding. Sleep and death are brothers.

When we are hurt the boundaries of our organism have been injured. Sleep disorders are located at the boundaries of consciousness. They can wear down our physical and mental health in a very short time. A healthy rhythm of waking and sleeping is essential for children and adolescents to get on with their task of growing up (Leber et al, 1990).

The rhythm of breathing with its incarnating and excarnating qualities finds symbolic expression in the forms of inward and outward winding spirals. "The spirals of incarnation and excarnation" (Vogel, 2007, 95) can bring balance to biological rhythms that were disturbed by trauma. They strengthen the life body and help children come to terms with their traumatic experiences.

Storytelling is another proven tool of emergency education. Nurturing images need to replace the horrific images of the disaster that have been burned into the body's memory. Folktales and fairy tales supply such healing images. The heroes in fairy tales grow inwardly when they have mastered a task or adventure. They become stronger. Identifying with these heroes can help children resolve their trauma (Hüther, 2008).

> Eight-year-old Katahira from Masushima has lost his grandparents in the tsunami. His father Hiroki (48) is worried: "He has not been able to concentrate since then and is fidgety. He doesn't listen at school and forgets everything."

Lack of concentration, inability to attend and memory problems are frequent results of the heightened excitation in cases of trauma. **Games** like Memory or Pick-up Sticks and **creative handicrafts** (Thomas, 2006) improve concentration and memory as well as fine motor movement.

Flexible fingers enhance the formation of synapses and neuronal networks in both halves of the brain. **Finger games** and string games (Dohm, 2009), **therapeutic handwork** (knitting, embroidering, crocheting, sewing) can therefore support the healing of trauma.

While the right half of the brain is in charge of emotions, creativity, body-awareness, and body perception, the right hemisphere is responsible for intellectuality, abstraction, reading, and speaking. The right side of the brain is mostly stimulated by visual perception and

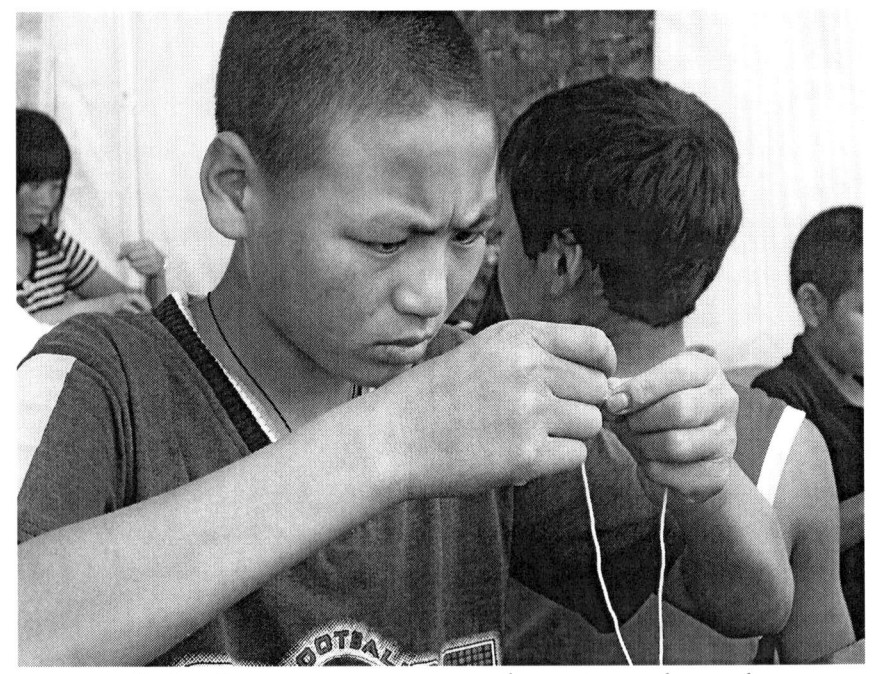

*String Games promote synapse formation and neural
networking between the two brain hemispheres
after the earthquake in China, June 2008*

by the left side of the body, while the left side is activated by auditory perception and the right half of the body. Neuronal transmission between both halves of the brain is enhanced when both hands are active and when the body's vertical and horizontal midlines are frequently crossed. Trauma disrupts the connection between the two halves of the brain.

String games improve the connection between the brain's hemispheres after trauma, because both hands are involved and need to cross over frequently to form the individual string patterns. String games also enhance the mobility and interaction of all the fingers, and they promote spatial orientation and the eye-hand coordination that is essential for any directed movement.

> Nine-year-old Mieko eventually joined the circle in the Tokohu Museum in Tagajo. Her inner frozenness melted visibly during the

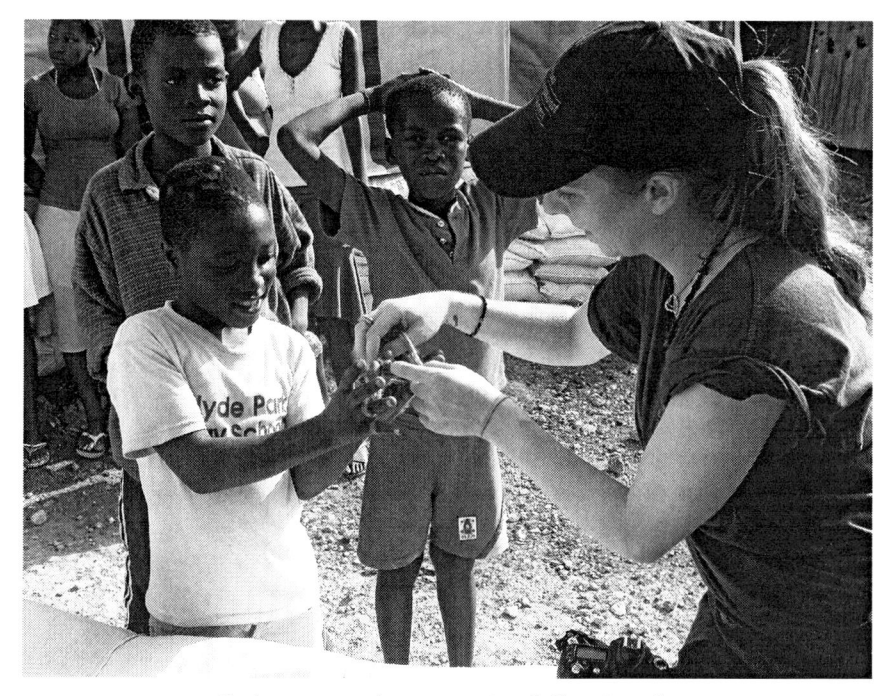

*String games in a tent city following the
devastating earthquake in Haiti, 2010*

activity, as life and warmth returned to her face. When asked by one of the Japanese educators if she would help paint name signs for the members of the emergency seminar, Mieko accepted and devoted herself cheerfully to the task.

Moments of joy increase the organism's readiness to heal. Research at the University of Pittsburgh has revealed that there is a connection between stress levels and susceptibility to colds (Servan-Schreiber, 2006, 78). Stress, anger, resentment, negative memories, etc. cause chaotic heart rhythms that—even if they only last for a few minutes—weaken the immune system for about six hours. The production of Immunoglobulin A (IgA) in the body's mucosal linings is clearly lowered after stressful experiences. As a result the organism is less resilient. The risk of infection is therefore much higher for trauma victims. Joy, compassion, and positive experiences, on the other hand, improve cardiac coherence. This, in turn, leads to the increased production of IgA and consequently greater resilience. Joy stimulates the powers of self-healing. Joy heals!

Support and Advice for Parents

> Since a massive earthquake shook the Chinese province of Sichuan, Tang Xiaohui (39) has lived in a tent city near Chuantindian. Like many other parents she lost her only child and cannot come to terms with her loss: "I was the first mother to trudge through the ruined town to the school. There was chaos everywhere. None of the teachers could speak because they were overwhelmed by what was happening around them. We dug and dug and dug. The smell of decay was noticeable on the first day. It took three days before the army found my maimed daughter. She was buried in a mass grave. My husband, who has not spoken since the disaster, gave our daughter a mobile phone into her grave!" Tang Xiaohui is crying.

In supporting trauma victims through their mourning one gets to know different stages and qualities of crying. Not all crying brings relief.

What Did We Do Wrong?

Trauma is contagious. Children, who did not directly experience a traumatic event, can be infected by the trauma of their parents. They experience what psychologists refer to as "secondary traumatization."

> Sixty-year-old Mohammaheiha El Samouni from Zeitoun in the Gaza Strip, a mother of seven, describes the problems her remaining children experienced when she was traumatized by the loss of two children: "I was fleeing to Gaza City with the rest of the family and did not see my children die. I still dream of my dead children. I can't believe they are dead. I keep seeing them. I keep meeting them in the streets."

Children often respond to traumatizing events with psychosomatic symptoms or behaviors, and this can be very challenging for parents and teachers.

> "My children are always afraid in the night. They cry and scream and wet their beds. Since the war my seven-year-old daughter is scared of everything!" says mother of three, Rana Zayed (24).

We have many similar reports from the Gaza Strip.

> Sahar Samouni (37), who has ten children, laments, "Most of the children are constantly arguing. They are *bolshie,* stubborn, and accept no rules at all! But the grown-ups are also stressed and aggressive. Everyone loses their temper very quickly."

Other parents report that their children no longer listen to them and even hit them. The parents are desperate because they cannot understand their children's behavior. They often beat their children out of despair. However, beating won't help the children to heal. "What did we do wrong?" asks Suleima (25), mother of a six-year-old, despondently.

Reports of regressive behaviors and self-harm among children are ubiquitous.

> Somaya El Sultan from Salatin says, "I had weaned my three-year-old son four months before the war. During the bombings he wouldn't stop asking for my breast and in the end I gave in. He still screams if I don't breastfeed him. He keeps shouting, 'we will be next!'" Another mother tells us how her four-year-old son bites the tips of his thumbs until they bleed.

Parents are in despair and urgently need help and advice. Love, affection, and safety, rhythm and rituals (a structured day, regular eating and sleeping rhythms), exercise and games (ball games, rope games, swings, circle games), artistic activities (painting, drawing, modeling, handicrafts), body contact (rhythmic *Einreibungen,* massage) and the nurturing of spiritual-religious feelings are essential tools in the work with traumatized children and youngsters.

It is good for parents to learn emergency techniques, such as breathing exercises to alleviate panic attacks or eye movement therapy to break up compulsive memories (flashbacks). These methods constitute stabilizing emergency interventions that can be carried out by parents in the absence of professionals.

It Is Not Your Response but the Event that Is Abnormal

> Three-year-old Madinur fell into a six-meter-deep hole when her family fled to Uzbekistan in 2010 during the pogroms in the southern Kyrgyz city of Osh. "Since then she has been wetting her bed again. She doesn't fall asleep unless I'm with her and she gets into a panic when she hears a loud noise. Since her fall she's also developed eczema in her left eye!" says her mother, a single parent.

Helping children and adolescents after disasters includes supporting their traumatized parents who are in urgent need of counseling and might require educational advice. These parents need assistance with resolving their own trauma because parents need to be mentally stable and inwardly calm so they can convey stability to their traumatized children. Parents need psycho-education (Landolt, 2004, 71ff.; Hausmann, 2006, 123) to help them understand what trauma is, how it is caused and what courses it may take. It is most important to understand that the symptoms of posttraumatic stress that appear in the first weeks after the disaster are not yet an illness. They are a normal response to abnormal events and, in the first instance, useful attempts of the organism to heal itself. Educational guidelines need to be worked out that can support parents in dealing with these traumatic responses. Such guidelines for emotional first aid must include the provision of affection, rhythm, rituals, movement, art, play, boundaries, and joy. If the initially normal responses to a traumatic event do not abate after weeks or months and posttraumatic disorders emerge, parents need to consult competent professionals.

Little Madinur from Osh and his mother received practical help. Children who have suffered bad falls can be helped if an attachment figure does gentle horse-trotting rhymes with them. The game is like an "attachment exercise" that allows children to build up new self-confidence in an unthreatening situation and to develop trust in the reliability of an attachment figure.

Emergency education, including training courses for parents, was carried out in Osato and Tagajo in Northern Japan and in Tokyo. Most parents say that they themselves have been fearful, edgy, and frustrated since the disaster. They cling to their children, are afraid to leave the house, and they suffer from psychosomatic symptoms. Many of them have developed asthma, allergies and, above all, rheumatism.

> One of the mothers can sleep only in the dining room since the earthquake. "We parents need help, too," says Minako (32). She has two children (2 years, 3 months). Both she and her children were buried in their house until soldiers rescued them three days later. "The children cried and clung to me all the time. I was distraught and felt so helpless. I still can't cope with everyday tasks. I am ashamed because I can't cope with my children." Katsonubo (35), who was not directly affected by the earthquake and tsunami, says that for weeks afterward he and his nine-year-old son Oki couldn't stop watching programs about the disaster shown on TV or on the internet. It was like an addiction. Oki has since developed a constant urge to urinate. He suffers from "secondary traumatization." Media reports can be traumatizing, too!

We often hear from parents that, after a catastrophe, their children initially showed no signs of trauma, as if nothing had happened. In these cases the first signs often appear only weeks later. We have also had reports of children who looked after their afflicted parents, comforting them and trying to give them emotional support. Research has shown that some children hide their trauma because they feel an irrational sense of guilt or shame. But they hide their own wounds also in order not to burden their parents with more worries. It is also known that children emulate the behavior of their sick parents, which can have long-term implications for their own development—they withdraw from their friends and therefore cannot gain wider social skills. They develop a weak sense of self-worth and find it very difficult to detach from their parents and gain independence.

Before we embarked on our emergency education intervention in Japan we were warned that, due to their cultural background, Japanese people would find it difficult to speak about their trauma. Direct questions after a person's wellbeing would be considered indiscrete if not invasive and would probably not be answered. We decided nevertheless to offer parents, who were severely traumatized themselves, psycho-educational guidance for their own relief and possibilities to share their trauma in groups. The sessions started with information about physical and psychological symptoms and possible behavioral changes in their social environment. People were able to speak about their own children and relatives and, in the end, were offered the opportunity to express their personal worries and needs. All offers of conversation were gratefully accepted within a few minutes and extensively utilized. What we Europeans found surprising was that many of the Japanese trauma victims were more affected by the suffering of their neighbors than by their own, often very difficult, fate.

Crisis Management Based on Emergency Education

Teachers are also traumatized after disasters. One of the most essential tasks of emergency education in crisis intervention—apart from the acute care for children and the counseling of parents—was to inform teachers and educators about the origin, course, and possible outcome of trauma and show them emergency education strategies for dealing with trauma-induced behaviors observed in children and youngsters.

Being a Teacher in the Face of the Apocalypse

> Dede is a 45-year-old English teacher who lives in a refugee camp in Sungai Batang at Lake Maninjau, a crater lake in Western Sumatra, Indonesia. "When the earthquake started I was very worried about my family. In couldn't find my fourteen-year-old daughter until the next day. No-one was hurt but I've had stomach problems ever since and often throw up."

Lorie (23), a teacher in Port-au-Prince, Haiti, speaks about her experiences following the major earthquake: "My older sister, who was eight months pregnant, and my little brother were on their way to my room to pick me up for dinner when the earthquake started. The three-story building collapsed instantly. All three of us were buried under the rubble. My sister screamed because she couldn't breathe. Then she died. People were running over the rubble outside. Every step crushed us even more. A man who was buried under the debris spoke to us. We spoke the Lord's Prayer. Hours later we were dug out. My brother's feet were jammed. The emergency services wanted to amputate his legs. I begged that they would make the effort to lift the concrete slab. Because I refused they left him behind to help others. Then they came back and actually managed to free my little brother. Fifteen people died in our house."

Sulfur (36), a teacher in Osh in Southern Kyrgyzstan, is suffering from the traumatic effects of the civil war. "Everything seems too much. I can't concentrate and since the tragic events I no longer enjoy teaching!" Her colleagues suffer from posttraumatic lack of motivation, persistent jumpiness, memory problems, panic attacks, and marital problems.

The teachers in Hongbai in the Chinese province of Sichuan are tormented by the trauma they suffered during the earthquake that destroyed many schools. They blame themselves. Things are made worse by the accusations of parents who lost their children and are looking for culprits. "Teachers who walked ahead of their pupils during the evacuation are accused of trying to save their own lives first," says teacher Xu Xingyou (33), "while teachers who walked behind their classes are blamed for not leading their pupils." He has received several death threats and is in constant fear of his life. Xu Xingyou finds the accusations against the teachers in Hongbai hard to bear: "I dug out a dead colleague. He lay stretched out over his children like a bridge to protect them!"

Now We Understand the Children and Ourselves Better

What we have said about the Japanese parents is equally true for teachers and educators. They are traumatized, too, and often unable to understand the trauma-induced behaviors of the children. They also

*Teacher training in various emergency
education measures, Tokyo, May 2011*

need to find their own stability again so they can support the children and adolescents in their care.

To ensure the continued success of the emergency education provided, local teachers, educators, and caregivers are, wherever possible, included in the interventions. We teach them how to apply emergency education in practice and they can experience the immediate effect of the measures used on the children. In the pedagogical debriefing sessions we hold they ask pertinent questions which often lead to professional discussions about the background and aims of the methods we use. In Onagawa, Ishinomaki, and Rifu it was possible to conduct effective training sessions on emergency education with the local teachers.

> "We are glad that we are better able to understand the children and ourselves, and that we have learned how to help the children in these difficult times to assimilate their horrific experiences," says Minako (25), a teacher at the primary school in Onogawa, after finishing the seminar.

At the Yojogi-Olympic Center in Tokyo around 100 Waldorf teachers and educators, anthroposophic doctors and therapists came together for a one-day seminar on emergency education. As well as practice sessions in emergency education and conversation groups on trauma, brief introductory talks were offered on the theory of traumatology and the possibilities of emergency education as crisis intervention.

In Tokyo it was also possible to train more than 70 anthroposophic teachers, educators, physicians, and therapists in an intensive course so that emergency teams could be set up for further assignments in the disaster area in the North of Japan.

The pedagogical interventions that are used to help traumatized children are based on the following trauma model: an initial brief period of shock is followed by a stress response phase that lasts several weeks. During this phase it will emerge whether or not the trauma could be resolved and integrated into the biography. Emergency education strives to stimulate and support this resolution process by dissolving physiological and emotional blockages. The overall aim is to activate the trauma victim's power of self-healing. The inner frozenness of the victim needs to melt so that the necessary grieving process that has been blocked can take its course and come to a conclusion. If this cannot be achieved, posttraumatic disorders (such as PTSD) can develop which, in the worst case, lead to permanent personality changes and the disruption of the victim's biography. Once posttraumatic disorders have emerged, emergency education can continue as a means of support, but the main focus will be on therapeutic interventions. The question remains as to how kindergartens, schools and care centers as well as the processes of teaching and learning should be designed so that they can competently address trauma-induced learning and behavioral disorders in children and adolescents. What can a special education for trauma victims look like? Two months after its black day, Japan had to confront these questions. For this too, our Japanese friends and colleagues needed to be prepared.

5

EMERGENCY EDUCATION AS THRESHOLD EDUCATION

AN ANTHROPOSOPHICALLY EXTENDED UNDERSTANDING OF DISASTER AND TRAUMA

We have so far described the multiple symptoms that may result from trauma. They include phobias, flashbacks, dissociative amnesia, and other dissociative disorders. In the work of Rudolf Steiner we find less common approaches that are based on a holistic spiritual view of human nature and of the world and that introduce us to an extended understanding of trauma. Chapter 5 looks at the phenomena surrounding traumatic events and their connection with human nature from the point of view of anthroposophic spiritual science.

PRENATAL TRAUMA

There are various kinds of stressful events that may cause trauma—natural disasters (earthquakes, droughts and famines, flooding, tornadoes, fires), accidental disasters (accidents, explosions, nuclear catastrophes) and incidents such as maltreatment, abuse, neglect, wars, crime, torture, displacement, flight, bullying, etc. If we include spiritual aspects we will discover even more causes for trauma that are, however, not taken into consideration by today's trauma research.

In 1901 Ellen Key published a book with the title *The Century of the Child*. In her introduction the author explained that she had felt she had to write the book after seeing a cartoon in a daily paper, depicting a vision of the coming century. It was the caricature "of a naked child that, descending down toward the earth, turns back horrified at the sight of a globe so studded with weapons that there is nowhere left to even set a foot" (Key, 2010/1901, 34).

What a gloomy vision; a child arrives from life before birth, intent on realizing his prenatal goals in an earthly incarnation, but is put off by the prevailing materialism that makes allowance for neither spirituality nor future development.

The souls of children who are on their way down to the earth will meet the souls of those who have just died and who are on their way to the spiritual world. What will they have to say to each other? What will the souls of those who have just died have to say to the incarnating souls about their life on earth? It is to be feared that the worries and hopes of the incarnating souls who have come down with their impulses for the future will be met mostly by the disappointed and frustrated souls of the recently deceased who found themselves unable to realize their life goals in a world governed by materialism.

In August 2011, around 20 million people were facing starvation in the Horn of Africa, due not only to widespread corruption, mismanagement, and climate change but also to people's insatiable greed. Big international speculators with pension funds worth billions of dollars and private investors looking for secure portfolios and profit maximization drove food prices so high that the poor could no longer afford their "daily bread." According to the FAO index, food prices rose by 39 percent and grain prices by 71 percent. "How is it possible that large pension funds and small investors gamble with the world food supplies? And that the question of how many people have to go hungry is ultimately decided at the stock exchanges in Chicago, New York or London?...High finance has turned a few screws and made the world's food an object of speculation" (Spiegel, 29 August 2011, 77). The food market has become a financial market that yields fast and bizarrely high profits. International financial markets have turned agricultural resources into big business and made "hunger a commodity" (ibid., 75).

The materialism of today's civilization has the potential to traumatize souls that are on their way to incarnation. If we view the situation with this spiritual dimension in mind we must also consider the possibility of prenatal trauma.

Trauma as a Borderline Experience

With the advances made in medicine it has become possible to reanimate people who have died. What these people experience at the threshold of death is unlike anything they have been familiar with before.

Dissociation: "The Unity of Thinking, Feeling, and Doing Is Broken Up"

Psychologists explain dissociation as a separation process. The actual event, the way it is perceived and the feelings or actions associated with the event become separated. As a result trauma sufferers may develop memory and perception disorders, tunnel vision, or lose their sense of reality.

Dissociation "is felt as being somewhere other than in one's body. It has been described…as 'feeling like I am on the ceiling looking down on myself'; or 'part of me is on the other side of the room'; or 'I just don't feel like I'm all here'" (Levine and Kline, 2007, 63). Affected persons often describe a feeling as if they were standing next to themselves.

> Some people "beam" themselves inwardly, away from the danger zone. Rather than be stuck in the crashed car they watch from a distance. They feel as if they were hovering above the scene…. Or the threatening event seems far away as if they were looking at it through a tunnel…. Their perception changes, they feel unreal. They experience time differently. Everything slows down. Split seconds seem like minutes or hours. While they are

propelled toward their certain doom, people might see important moments of their life rising before their inner eye, like a film. (Fischer, 2006, 13)

Psychopathology refers to this kind of inner separation as dissociation. "It involves the fragmentation of a person's thinking, feeling, perception and behavior within their temporal and spatial context" (Krüsmann, Müller-Cyran, 2005, 49). Dissociation always has to do with the falling apart of developmental levels, such as a person's physiological and intellectual maturity or their intellectual-physiological and emotional-social development. Trauma can cause this kind of dissociation.

Near-Death Research:
"Trauma Can Evoke Near-Death Experiences"

Near-death research was founded in the United States as a scientific discipline when Dr. Raymond Moody, inspired by his former teacher, the American physician George Ritchie, began to collect reports of near-death experiences. Since then more such reports have been collected worldwide (Brinkley and Perry, 1994; van Lommel, 2009; Messner, 1987; Moody, 1977; Roszell, 1993; Ritchie, 1995; Ritchie and Sherrill, 2004; Zaleski, 1993). In his first publication on the subject Moody pointed out that no two experiences were the same but that they all shared the same features, for instance, at the threshold of death people see their inner life as separate from external events, and they perceive their own body as from the outside. Another common and important phenomenon is the panoramic life review. Reanimation is experienced as a "falling down" into one's body through a black tunnel or shaft.

Interestingly, the trauma symptoms described earlier resemble the phenomena known from near-death research. How can this be explained?

The Connection between the Members of the Human Organization Is Loosened.
"The Change of Consciousness at the Threshold of Death."

At the threshold of death our ether body, astral body, and "I" become detached from our physical body. As a result our consciousness changes because the state of our mind is dependent on their interaction.

When all four members of our organization are integrated we have either day or night consciousness. Depending on the intensity of the connection between the "I" and the other members, our day or night consciousness assumes various degrees. When the "I" becomes detached from the fabric of the other members, our consciousness becomes dreamlike. We are in deep sleep or in a state of night consciousness when the astral body also becomes detached from the rest of the organization. It is only in death that the ether body withdraws from its lifelong connection with the physical body.

According to Anthroposophy, the members of our organization become partly detached when we are in a state of shock. The connection between them is disrupted and the "I" is cast out. As a result we experience a change of consciousness. The partial or complete detachment of the ether body from the physical body can elicit phenomena similar to those known from near-death experiences.

Panoramic Life Reviews

When the ether body becomes detached after death it reveals itself as the carrier of our memory. The I no longer actively brings back individual memories, but the memories flash simultaneously before our inner eye, either chronologically, like in a film, or as a panoramic review.

Trauma sufferers can experience a similar loosening of the life body including panoramic reviews. Trauma can be a partial death experience.

The compulsive memories (flashbacks) and dissociative amnesia that can manifest in traumatized persons are also the result of pathological changes in the interaction of the members of our organization.

It is important to know that such a partial detachment of the ether body or other members of our organization in the aftermath of trauma may also occur in particular organs. It could happen that the etheric forces of the lung become suddenly detached through trauma and cause compulsive behaviors. A compulsive repetitive process that rises up from the respiratory tract forces itself onto the soul. Compulsive repetitive thoughts, feelings, and impulses are like an ongoing inhalation process, while compulsive actions are like an ongoing exhalation process (Treichler, 1993a, 351). Processes that are biologically vital become destructive when, for pathological reasons, they are moved to the soul level.

A Changed Perception of Time and Space: "Losing One's Footing"

While we need a physical body to experience space, it is our life body (ether body) that gives us time awareness. It forms a kind of time body within us. Vitality is closely connected with time-related processes such as development, regeneration, rhythms, and so on.

The fact that dissociation causes a person to experience time and place differently is, anthroposophically speaking, due to changes that occur in the interaction between the levels of the human organization that are caused by traumatic shock.

Desynchronization and Rhythmic Disorders: "Life Is Falling Apart"

Trauma can disturb the rhythms of the threefold human organism in many ways and cause disorders in the rhythm of forgetting and remembering, digestive problems, eating disorders, etc.

Inner desynchronization is one possible cause for rhythmic disorders. When systems of the rhythmic organization are no longer attuned to each other we may see symptoms of neurovegetative dystonia as a result. External desynchronization occurs when inner and outer rhythms are no longer in harmony, as happens, for instance, in the case of jetlag; the organism shows signs of crisis that also affect the soul life and may manifest in inner restlessness, malaise, and low energy levels.

Sleeping and eating disorders may occur, too. They are not illnesses "but…symptoms of physical, psychic, and mental difficulties. Sleeplessness therefore can be caused by physical illness, psychic imbalance, or mental one-sidedness" (Bub-Jachens, 1997, 32).

From the point of view of Anthroposophy, rhythmic disorders occur when the interplay between the levels of our organization are disturbed as a result of traumatic shock. When the connection between these levels is loosened the affected person may develop a number of vegetative, psychosomatic, psychological, and mental disorders.

This would explain why rituals, structure, and daily rhythms can help to readjust and harmonize the interplay of the levels of our organization and promote healing.

TRAUMA LEADS TO UNEXPECTED THRESHOLD EXPERIENCES

In 2008, the French apnea diver Guillaume Néry (29) became free-diving champion. The best South Pacific pearl divers can reach a depth of 45 meters. In 1960, sports physicians still thought it was impossible to dive deeper than 50 meters. Néry's record now lies at 115 meters—without the use of scuba gear. He has learned to outsmart his breathing reflex and can hold his breath for eight minutes, despite the effort needed to resurface wearing a weight belt. Néry's pulmonary volume is 10 liters, four liters more than that of the average person. At 115 meters the water pressure equals 13 kilograms per square centimeter of body. Lungs are compressed to the size of oranges. One cannot use a diving mask because the reduced pressure might suck out the eyeballs. "It's a trip to a death zone" (Spiegel, August 8, 2011, 134). Néry is fascinated by the profound blueness of the underwater world. "At this depth the gases in the blood dissolve which makes me feel slightly high or inebriated.… I feel free in a way that I never could on land" (Ibid., 134). Néry spent 14 years training, practicing thousands of dives to adjust his body to the conditions at a depth of 115 meters. Untrained, his body would not withstand the extreme conditions and the threshold experiences of the unfamiliar environment.

The experiences at the threshold of the spiritual world that Rudolf Steiner described are no less extreme or less dangerous. We need to be prepared for them, too. In ancient times, suitable individuals chosen to be initiates had to prepare themselves by undergoing a path of inner development.

When we are healthy our soul forces are kept in harmony while we are awake during the day. Our thinking, feeling, and impulses for action are held together by our physical organization. When we dream there is already less coherence. The levels of our organization become detached when we are sleeping. Soul and "I" leave the enlivened body to an extent, especially in the head area. Dreams cannot be steered consciously. The "I" loses its power over the feeling life.

Steiner knew from his spiritual-scientific research that a healthy soul life relies on the natural, unconscious coherence of the soul forces of thinking, feeling, and will. This coherence is radically disrupted when we approach the threshold of the spiritual world. The levels of our organization become detached.

> Great changes definitely occur.... These changes are connected with certain evolutionary processes taking place in the three fundamental forces of the soul—willing, feeling, and thinking.... The relationship between these is determined by higher cosmic laws.... These seemingly simple connections between thinking, feeling, and willing are the foundation upon which, if we survey it, we find that our whole life is built. We even consider the interconnectedness of these powers of thinking, feeling, and willing—based, as they are, on the laws of human nature—to be a prerequisite for a "normal" life. (Steiner, 1994, CW 10, 176)

When we reach the threshold of the spiritual world, or the threshold of death, the interconnectedness of thinking, feeling, and will is dissolved. The soul forces separate and the "I" has to hold them together consciously. "At this point in our spiritual evolution, the organs of thinking, feeling, and willing function separately, quite independently of one another. Their interconnection is thus no longer regulated by their own inherent laws, but by the individual's awakened higher consciousness" (Ibid., 178). As we cross the threshold of consciousness to the suprasensory world, our "I" must be able to establish and maintain the connection between our soul forces. "During suprasensory observation, thinking, feeling, and willing do not remain three forces radiating from their common center in the 'I' of the person in question. They become independent beings—three separate personalities, so to speak. The individual 'I' must become that much stronger, because rather than simply having to impose order on three forces, it must now guide and direct three beings" (Steiner, 1997, CW 13, 353).

Separation processes may occur if we are unable to hold our soul forces together and direct them: "We must train ourselves and acquire the inner strength to hold the three elements of our soul life—thinking, feeling, and willing—together with our 'I.' Otherwise we would split into three personalities" (Steiner, 1964, CW 192, 64).

The Danger of the Split Personality:
"When the Soul Life Becomes Dissociated"

When we embark on a path of inner development, the levels of our organization become detached. Our soul forces come apart and the connection between thinking, feeling, and will is disrupted. These kinds of changes can be caused by various circumstances, even when we don't consciously try to achieve them. If we are not prepared, however, we will find ourselves exposed to spiritual threshold experiences without being able to cope with them. A haunting description of the consequences of unprepared initiation can be found in Friedrich Schiller's poem "The Veiled Image at Sais." Trauma is such an "unprepared threshold experience" (Kaiser, 2011, 3).

When, at the threshold of the spiritual world, our physical organization can no longer hold the soul forces together and they drift apart, our ordinary consciousness dissolves and our own, as well as other people's, faculties of thinking, feeling, and will appear as objective, real beings: "These figures are real; there are as many of them in the spiritual world as there are individual human souls.... We must know that, what is usually just a weak shadow in our soul, will now come toward us as a living, differentiated trinity of three beings" (Steiner, 1997, CW 147, 116).

When trauma leads us to the threshold of death or to a near-death experience, the natural connection between thinking, feeling, and will may suddenly be torn apart without the "I" being able to control these soul forces. The danger of a split personality arises. "Such a separation of thinking, feeling, and willing can easily lead us to deviate from the proper human path of development in three ways. Such a deviation occurs when the links connecting the three forces of the soul are destroyed before higher consciousness and its understanding are sufficiently advanced to be able to take the reins and lead the now separated forces in the right way to a free, harmonious working together. The achievement of higher consciousness is necessary because, as a rule, the three forces do not develop equally in every phase of a person's life. In one person thinking may be more developed than feeling and willing, while in another feeling or willing may be predominant. As long as the connection between thinking, feeling, and willing remains regulated by the higher laws of the cosmos, however, such developmental discrepancies do not cause any disturbing irregularities in the higher sense. If will predominates in a person, for example, then the cosmic laws ensure that other forces counterbalance it and keep it from becoming excessive" (Steiner, 1994, CW 10, 179f.).

When such will people cross the threshold to the spiritual world unprepared and their soul forces separate, "Then the regulating influence of feeling and thinking on the will ceases, and the will, now no longer held in check, constantly impels us on to tremendous performances of power.... Our will can run rampant. It can overwhelm us, so that our feeling and thinking sink into complete powerlessness and we become slaves, scourged by our will. As a result, we can become violent in character, rushing from one unbridled action to the next" (Ibid., 180).

If the feeling dominates and is unbridled, another, no less pathological, state of soul will ensue: "A person inclined to revere others, for instance, can then become so completely dependent on them that he or she loses the will and ability to think. Instead of higher knowledge, such a person's lot is the most pitiful inner emptiness and impotence. If the natural tendency of our feelings is toward piety and religious exaltation, on the other hand, we can fall into raptures of religious self-gratification"(Ibid., 180f.).

If the thinking prevails when we cross the threshold and terrorizes feeling and will, the outcome will be equally pathological: "This produces a contemplative nature, but one that is closed in upon itself and hostile to life. For a person of such a nature the world has meaning only insofar as it provides objects to satisfy a boundless desire for wisdom. Thoughts no longer stir such a person to action or feelings. Instead, such people become indifferent and cold" (Ibid., 181).

The fundamental human soul forces, when torn apart and individualized, unfold a one-sided, distorted dynamic of their own, entering into inadequate, pathological relationships with each other. "Thus there are three ways in which we can go astray.... We can fall into willful violence, into sentimental luxuriating in feelings, or into a cold, loveless striving after wisdom" (Ibid., 181).

The separation process described may give rise to various psychopathologies (Straube and Hasselberg, 1994, 28ff.). Fixated ideas combined with unbridled will forces, for instance, can produce all kinds of compulsive behaviors. When the feelings tie themselves to the will we tend to see substance abuse as a consequence. When the driven will impulses connect themselves to the thinking there is a danger of hysteria, and if swaying feelings hold on to our thinking, our thought life will become disoriented.

At the Threshold: Meeting the "Monster Trauma"

Steiner portrayed the threshold situation, the human being standing at the abyss, artistically in the colored windows of the Goetheanum in Dornach, Switzerland. Some of these window motifs are relevant in the context of trauma and shall therefore be briefly described. Opposite the entrance to the Main Auditorium, in the west of the building, we find the "red window," which has the form of a triptych with a larger central part and two smaller side parts. In the middle part of the red window we see the face of the spiritual researcher who has come to the threshold to the spiritual world on a path of conscious inner development. Two of his spiritual organs of perception, also known as chakra or lotus flowers, have been activated—one on his forehead, the other in the region of the larynx.

The left side of the triptych shows the human being at the threshold to the suprasensory world: "He stands before the abyss. Out of the abyss terrifying beasts appear. They have been created by human beings. Fear, hatred, and doubt are not just soul stirrings that can accompany our willing, feeling and thinking. They are real beings that we need to overcome" (Hartmann, 1971, 25). When we reach the threshold of the suprasensory world, three animals will appear from out of the depths. They are distorted images of our own soul forces; the dirty-red beast with split mouth and slouching attitude is an image of the doubt that lives in our thinking; the second beast, mocking, represents our feelings of hatred; and the blue beast with crooked back stands for will-paralyzing fears.

> Everything that chains us to the earth and to its transient life and that we have to leave behind as transient, appears to us there...in the image of the distorted bull.... What usually creates harmony of will and feeling in our soul appears to us in relation to our sins of omission in the image of the distorted lion. And everything that passes us by because of the sins of omission we commit in our thinking,...is revealed in the image of the distorted eagle. These three images are permeated by our own distorted image.... Three distorted images and one distorted image of ourselves! We can see

from the way these three images relate to each other how much we still have to work on ourselves." (Steiner, 1962, CW 119, 116)

We find the "beasts of the abyss" also in literature as inner experiences on the esoteric path. In his *Divine Comedy*, Dante described the life-threatening encounter with the "beasts at the gates of hell"—lion, leopard and she-wolf—as "going astray in the dark wood."

The right side of the triptych shows the human being after crossing the threshold, having overcome the abyss. The "beasts of the abyss" have been conquered and are sliding away at the lower end of the window. "Once he has overcome the abyss he can turn toward the spirit sun" (Ibid., 116). When the visitor crosses the threshold and steps into the Main Auditorium he will see eight colored windows in its north and south walls, depicting further experiences in the spiritual world.

In a way, the left side of the red window shows the situation of the trauma sufferer too. The shock has brought him to a near-death experience and he now stands—unprepared—at the gates to the suprasensory world. The soul forces of thinking, feeling, and will drift apart. The "I" is unable to hold them together or direct them. The "beasts of the abyss" appear as fear, hatred, and doubt in the soul of the traumatized person.

The double: "Encounter with the shadow"

> To this day she doesn't know why. Six times Nadia stabbed her friend with a knife. Now the sixteen-year-old appears in court. No-one was able to control her, not even she herself.... "I don't know why I did it," Nadia says. She had not thought anything of it. Hadn't thought anything when she ran a three-inch knife into her friend's chest?... She remembers two stabs. There were at least six. (Eissele, 2007)

> The pretty girl with the dark hair and earnest face sits in her prison cell. She writes letters. Her handwriting is like a little child's. She decorates the envelopes with colorful patterns. She is calm, thoughtful, introverted—not many people know this side of her.

The red stained glass at the West entrance of the Goetheanum in Dornach, Switzerland; designed by Rudolf Steiner (1913–14); executed by Asya Turgenjewa (Hartmann, Goetheanum Stained-Glass Windows)

Then there is the other Nadia; she roars, goes on rampages, wears army clothes, chain-smokes, drinks Vodka till she drops, calls the police officers "freaks," and tries to kick one of them in the crotch.
"There are two worlds inside Nadia," says her former teacher.... Angelic face—and incredible anger; she had never understood it. (Ibid.)

It happened on June 31, 2006, in the city center of Karlsruhe in Germany; Nadia stabbed her best friend Nicole to death. Such homicides happen frequently. And numerous attempts have been made to explain the inconceivable.

Steiner described a shocking event that takes place at the threshold of the spiritual world once the soul forces of thinking, feeling, and

Emergency Education as Threshold Education

will have separated. "Among the most important experiences in the ascent to higher worlds are the encounters with the so-called guardian of the threshold.... We meet the first [guardian] when the connection between willing, thinking, and feeling in the finer (astral and ether) bodies begins to loosen" (Steiner, 1994, CW 10, 184).

The encounter with the distorted, horrible, ghost-like being who stands guard at the threshold to the spiritual world is horrifying.

> If we leave the physical body without preparation we will not be nobler and purer than we were when we inhabited a physical form. We are beings with all the imperfections that we took on as karma. All that remains invisible as long as the temple of your body encloses our ether and astral bodies and our "I." However, the moment we leave the physical body with our higher members it becomes visible. All the leanings and passions we still carry with us from what happened in earlier incarnations appear before our eyes.... Everything we are capable of doing in the world, any harm we did to others that we will need to make up for in the future, is incorporated into our astral and ether bodies when we leave our physical body behind. We meet ourselves naked, as it were, in soul and spirit.... It is at this moment that we realize how far away we are from the perfection we are striving to achieve. (Steiner, 1982, CW 113, 40f.)

Meeting the double means meeting our own self, our "shadow" (Kast, 2004). Rudolf Steiner described the guardian of the threshold, among other things, as the double we meet on crossing the threshold to the spiritual world. In this double, all our errors, wrongdoings, and imperfections assume a distorted, demonic form. This shadow side only emerged in the course of our earth evolution. It is the part of us that has distanced itself from our light side. From incarnation to incarnation we must transform this demonic being into one of shining beauty through atonement and reformation. We must dissolve and integrate the "shadow."

Again, we find examples of the phenomenon that Rudolf Steiner described as the "guardian of the threshold" in literature, for instance in Franz Kafka's "Before the Law," Oscar Wilde's *Picture of Dorian*

Gray and in Dostoyevsky's *The Double*. In his analytical psychology, C. G. Jung refers to the double as the "shadow" (Kast, 2007, 52ff.).

Robert Menasse (2001) described in his novel *Die Vertreibung aus der Hölle* (Expulsion from Hell) how our double, or "shadow," can be projected to the outside. His story is set in Austria in the 1960s and 70s. Victor Abravanel, a pupil in a boarding school, who is not aware of his own Jewish origins, joins in the bullying of Jewish children. The following scene describes him abusing Feldstein, a fellow pupil:

> Victor had punched Feldstein in the face. He had heard the bone in his nose crack, felt the pain of Feldstein's teeth on his knuckles, just once he had wanted to slam him, just one strike, he would be beaten up forever if he did not prove, this once, that he, too, could strike. He had been thrashed too often, he just had to fight back once. So he struck, the smallest—helpless little Feldstein. Just one punch, but what then happened he would never forget; he saw the ugliness that pain created, the grotesque face of his humiliated victim, the dehumanized expression of his intimidated, battered victim seemed to confirm to him that it was right to frighten, harm, humiliate, kick, ridicule him so one just had to smash his face. Suddenly, all Victor wanted to do was keep hitting the grotesque face because it horrified him, he wanted it to go away. He, who was weak, did not quit hitting, he thrashed the weakest, he was out of his mind, it was no longer a human being he smashed, it was a creature, how could a human being be so ugly, so repulsive, so crude was the pleading, or whatever that was in his eyes, so distorted were his features, suddenly it was a smudgy thing that one could hammer the soul out of, only slime and blood and shit one would hammer out of this creature, one had to stamp on him until the shit disappeared, finally disappeared in the cracks of the floor. It had to disappear, it could not be there, it must not have a place in the world, not as long as there were eyes that had to see this, with hands and feet Victor tried to extinguish this kid, this grimace, until he was pulled away, held, still writhing, twitching in the hands of those who were holding him back. (Menasse, 2001, 33)

Victor, traumatized himself by the violence he had experienced, meets his own double which he projects into the weaker Feldstein. By fighting the unbearable, grotesque, distorted creature in the other he tries to extinguish it. The scene can be described "from a psychological point of view as the extraversion of the perpetrator-ego-state of a massively traumatized person who recognizes himself in the grotesquely distorted face of his victim and who despises himself for his weakness in the image of the other and tries to destroy himself" (Peichl, 2007, 227).

Scenes like the one described by Menasse happen daily in pedestrian zones and tube stations. Extreme trauma can trigger threshold experiences and encounters with one's shadow. This shadow is often projected into another person where the perpetrator fights it in order to destroy it. In the state of posttraumatic excitation the boundaries between I and you become blurred. Many murders can therefore be interpreted as repressed suicides.

Sixteen-year-old Nadia from Karlsruhe probably had such a threshold experience that she was not prepared for. She also met her shadow.

Fears at the Threshold: "The Existential Fear of Extinction"

The trauma-induced semiconscious meeting with the shadow at the threshold can elicit states of extreme anxiety. Rudolf Steiner mentioned a center of destruction within us that we are not conscious of, where all matter is being destroyed (Treichler, 1995, 78). In the biochemical processes of the digestive system matter is indeed being destroyed. There are of course no moral implications to this nutritional process that constitutes the foundation of our physical existence. But in states of traumatic shock, such processes that should only take place at the physical level, are transferred to the soul level where they can cause (self-)destructive mental illnesses.

Because the members of our organization become separated after trauma, the etheric forces associated with our inner center of destruction become active—and partly conscious—in our soul life. Etheric forces from our organs rise to consciousness where they are perceived as destructive forces. They trigger massive existential fears that begin to dominate the trauma victim (Ibid., 78).

Trauma Involves Feelings of Guilt and Shame

Yoko (27) lost her eight-year-old son in the tsunami of 11 March 2011. He was a pupil at the Ookawa primary school in Ishinomaki in Northern Japan. Yoko blames herself. She is convinced that her son would still be alive if she had not separated from her husband six years ago. She would not have had to work, she says, and would have picked up her son from school.

It might strike us as almost absurd that trauma victims should develop feelings of guilt and shame although they are the ones who experienced violence. Why do children who have suffered unspeakable harm feel ashamed or guilty?

Perpetrator Introjects: The Demon inside the Victim

In August 1973, two heavily armed robbers held more than sixty people hostage in a bank in Stockholm. Four staff members were kept by the kidnappers in a small vault for 131 hours before they were rescued by police. A rather strange phenomenon was then observed in the hostages; they were more afraid of the police than of their captors. They even felt grateful toward their kidnappers because they had not killed them.

Psychologists refer to the phenomenon as "Stockholm syndrome." The syndrome has been observed frequently in all parts of the world and is thought to arise from the extreme stress that victims as well as perpetrators are exposed to in hostage situations. It has three main characteristics: "The hostages have positive feelings toward their captors; the hostages have negative feelings toward the police or authorities; the captors develop positive feelings for their hostages. In this interpretation the bonding is seen as a way of coping with extreme stress, for victims and perpetrators" (Peichl, 2007, 236).

According to one hypothesis in trauma research the victims are imitating the perpetrators (Howell, 2002, 921ff.). Owing to the extreme violence, the victims are exposed to and their inability to integrate the experience, their "I"-functions break down and one speaks of "imitation as taking on the perspective of the other owing to identity diffusion" (Ibid., 224). Trauma research refers to this kind of imitation as "perpetrator introject" (Fischer and Riedesser, 1999).

Perpetrator introjects have far-reaching consequences for the victims: "Dwelling so intensely on the destructive intentions of another person at whose mercy you are entirely, putting yourself inwardly in his place in order to sense his intentions so you can better protect yourself—all this will leave deep intrapsychic traces. The other begins to live in you, as role model, as a model of interaction, as a perpetrator introject, as an imitation" (Peischl, 2007, 224). The souls of traumatized children are harassed by a destructive power, as if the perpetrator were always present and they begin to imitate the perpetrator in their relationship with other people.

These "perpetrator-ego-states" (ibid.) therefore have the effect that trauma victims become perpetrators, usually as the intrapsychic result of a relationship that they were unable to escape. The power behavior and subjection behavior that the victims alternate between can be seen as parts of the same "trauma template" (ibid., 225). "The violently abused child does not have two working models, one in which he is a terrorized victim and another in which he is gleefully sadistic. Rather, these are two sides of one and the same working model. The intense and effective ways in which abused children can be aggressive toward others are explained as resulting from the same relational model in which the child suffers as a victim. The working model compels the child to be not only a victim in relationship after relationship, but also, in other ways or in other relationships, a victimizer" (Prior, 1996, 91).

From an anthroposophic point of view, perpetrator introjects can affect any of the levels of our fourfold organization. "The more unconscious and concealed the moral transgressions the more deeply traumatizing they are. They can cause shifts within the astral sphere.... The trauma shifts the powers of the astral body in that the inferior feelings that the aggressor ought to have regarding his actions...are transferred to the other person" (Grill, 2010, 270ff.).

There are moral transgressions that are seen as permissible acts by a particular culture or civilization even though they are extremely immoral. Slavery, racism, torture, or exploitative economic systems were not always considered to be ethically wrong. These forms of moral transgressions are not necessarily perceived consciously by individuals and work as introjects in our life or etheric organization where, in the long term, they manifest as dispositions for certain illnesses, especially of the metabolic system. Cancer can therefore possibly be seen as the long-term result of such traumatic introjections.

Introjections can also affect the physical organization where they damage and destroy, as foreign bodies, the spiritual archetypes and forms that underlie our physical organism. Political and religious fundamentalism, if paired with manipulation and suggestion, can have this kind of destructive potential.

In an essay on the spiritual dimension of human beings ("*Die geistige Dimension des Menschen? Zur Entwicklung der medizinischen Anthropologie im 20. Jahrhundert*"; Selg, 2011b, 35ff.), Peter Selg asks about the role physicians played in the medical crimes committed under the Nazis, such as enforced sterilization and abortion, euthanasia, and experiments on human beings. "German physicians were standing at the selection ramps of concentration and extermination camps where the decision was made as to whether someone would die immediately in the gas chambers (or be temporarily admitted to a 'labor camp'). In a veritable 'synthesis of physician and executioner' and on an industrial scale these physicians decided over life or death" (Ibid., 55).

While the mass killings in the extermination camps were kept secret, the topic of euthanasia was less strictly guarded. "A degree of calculated connivance was not altogether unwelcome despite the official secrecy about the euthanasia killings. In the case of child euthanasia it was even part of the system, at least with regard to parents; the intention was to get the population used to the idea of a targeted elimination of life that was 'not worth living' so they would ultimately consent to such healthcare measures.... This was, after all, the project of a highly advanced medical elite, and the still backward population was to be gradually brought up to the humanitarian standard of that elite" (Dörner, 2001, 55f.).

While the official medical fraternity in Germany appeared aghast at the medical crimes, they saw them as the ethical aberrations of individuals and rejected any responsibility for them. The head of the Institute of History at Düsseldorf University, Alfons Labisch, on the other hand, put the medical crimes of the Nazis in a societal context.

> Nazi medicine was...in no way a historical accident perpetrated by low, criminal figures.... Modern medicine looks to scientific medicine for certainty regarding medical decisions, in individual as well as public healthcare. Since the turn of the 20th century this thinking has included the entire field of reproduction hygiene, eugenics or racial hygiene with its open boundaries regarding the question of race. There was no social group at the time that would not have dealt positively with the question of eugenics....The leading Nazi physicians saw the healthcare policies of National Socialism as integral to the scientific direction of modern medicine....They considered the medical interventions to be scientific, therapeutic and ethically justified and therefore as imperative. Nazi medicine autonomously legitimized and executed the biologistic society model of National Socialism. National Socialism and its medicine are inherent to the project of modernity. (Labisch, 2001, 58f.)

Nazi ideology with its image of the human being is political and pseudo-religious fundamentalism that has manipulated millions of people. It can be said that the perpetrator-introjects in this context have harmed the spiritual archetype of the human physical organization. This harm will manifest in dispositions for illnesses, especially of the neurosensory system, such as severe dementia. "Our time has generally a more or less traumatizing effect at this level, even though we might as individuals not be aware of that" (Grill, 2010, 271).

During perpetrator interjection the aggressor's feelings of guilt and shame are also transferred to the victim (Levi, 1993, 79ff.).

Perpetrators sense subconsciously that their wrongdoing is unacceptable to the higher self and the spiritual world. The deed, which manifests instantly in their Shadow Being, sets them back in their inner development and isolates them in the suprasensory world after death. Perpetrators also have feelings of shame and guilt in their innermost soul, but they can keep these sentiments and their consequences at bay by projecting them onto their victims.

The guilt and shame of trauma victims are therefore more than just consequences of personal wrongdoing. "The traumatized person carries within him a part of the perpetrator or even of a collective stream, that is alien to him and that he is, biographically, not responsible for, but that he takes on as a result of external circumstances" (Ibid., 268).

The Anthroposophic View of Guilt and Shame

In his book, *An Outline of Esoteric Science* (1997, CW 13), Steiner presents the anthroposophic concept of shame, relating it to the encounter with the "guardian of the threshold," as an aspect of our own double, at the threshold of the spiritual world.

> But if we delve into ourselves and hold up certain character traits for inspection without deceiving ourselves, either we will be in a position to correct them or we will be unable to do so in our present situation. In this latter instance, a feeling that we must describe as "shame" creeps into our souls. (Ibid., 357)

Aside from the outwardly noticeable shame, that is a kind of self-protection from other people, Rudolf Steiner describes another, intrapsychic sense of shame that we are not consciously aware of.

> Shame, therefore, is a force that impels us to conceal something within us and not allow it to become outwardly perceptible. If we give this due consideration, we will understand why spiritual research ascribes much more wide-ranging effects to an inner soul experience that is very closely related to the feeling of shame. This research reveals a type of hidden shame in the depths of the soul,

a shame that we do not become conscious of in our physical, sensory life." (Ibid., 358)

This hidden shame serves as self-protection against our own consciousness.

> It prevents a person's innermost being from appearing to that person as a perceptible image. If this feeling were not there, we would confront a perception of what we are in truth. We would not only have inner experiences of our ideas, feelings, and will; we would also perceive them just as we perceive stones, animals, and plants. This feeling conceals us from ourselves, and at the same time it conceals the entire world of soul and spirit. (Ibid., 358)

If we were confronted with our own shadow without being able to cope with it, this would have a devastating effect for our self-experience:

> And in fact, this concealed feeling acts like a great benefactor of human beings, because any powers of judgment, feeling life, or character we acquire without spiritual scientific training do not make us capable of standing up to the perception of our own nature in its true form without further preparation. Perceiving this would deprive us of all our self-esteem, self-confidence, and self-awareness. (Ibid., 359)

Shame Is More than the Consequence of Individual Guilt

When the barbarity of the Nazis had come to an end in 1945 and the true dimension of the cultural disaster became apparent, a passionate debate ensued about the collective guilt of the German people. Theodor Heuss, the first German president after the war, rejected the collective-guilt thesis, introducing the concept of "collective shame" instead. According to Heuss, shame is more than the consequence of individual guilt. "Shame can be felt representatively and it can actively support the process of overcoming. In doing so, shame becomes a moral-spiritual process" (Schad, 1979, 751).

From the anthroposophic point of view, shame serves to protect ourselves from other people and from our own self-awareness. It is much more than just a feeling we develop after having done wrong. "The feeling life seeks to conceal itself in our body and become invisible to the surroundings. The shamefulness, which slips down to the emotional levels of the sentient body, continues to affect the physiological life processes, making the blood of our physical body rise up to our head and into our cheeks so that we blush; as if the soul was creating a protective shield made of blood to hide behind" (Ibid., 750f.).

Trauma has been described above as an experience of shock and therefore as a partial near-death experience. Trauma has the effect that the three higher levels of our organization are partially torn from their physical foundation and we approach the threshold of the spiritual world where we first meet our own double or "shadow." The shame that is hidden in our soul and the shame that is noticeable on the outside shroud our self-image and prevent us from experiencing our own self without preparation, since such an experience would lead to a breakdown of our self-confidence, self-esteem, and self-awareness that would have profound implications for our mental health.

Trauma also belongs to aspects of ourselves that we are not ready to meet without preparation. It is part of our shadow being and needs to be concealed for our protection. This is why trauma is accompanied by shame. Shame can consequently be seen as an active spiritual-moral process of protection and coping that is much more than just a sensation of personal guilt.

Traumatization through Elemental Beings

Elemental beings are an important part of the imagery of folktales of many cultures—gnomes, who live among rocks and roots; undines, or mermaids, who are active in the various manifestations of the watery element; the sylphs and sprites of the air; and the salamanders, who live in fire and warmth. These beings are connected with the four elements; they act as beings of earth, water, air, and fire. Ogres are images of unrestrained natural forces; elves help the plants grow. In folktales, these elemental beings are often enchanted and waiting to be released by human beings.

Elemental Nature Forces

In earlier times the connection between humans and elementals was part of everyday life. North American Native Americans and First Nations people have tended to see natural beings at work in every spring and landscape, even entire regions. The Germanic tribes heard elemental beings speak in the rustling of leaves or in the gurgling of a river.

In over fifty lecture cycles Rudolf Steiner called our attention to the fact that the forces or "natural laws," that we now have only abstract concepts of, are actual beings that are, in a way, enchanted or bound to nature or to the movements of planets where they are now at work (Steiner, 2001, CW 102; 1974, CW 136; 1978, CW 230). Rudolf Steiner referred to these diverse astral-etheric forces as "elemental beings."[1]

Unredeemed Nature Beings

During our earthly life we are connected with nature and the beings active in it. These beings are waiting to be released. If we strive for knowledge and for the ennobling of our feelings and will impulses, we can set these beings free from their task and from their banishment to the material world. Rudolf Steiner divides the elemental nature beings into four groups.

The first group is the **nature beings** we know from folktales. When we look at nature these beings enter into us and remain in us until we die.

---
1. Even though Steiner's indications regarding the elemental forces that are at work in nature and in humanity might well meet with reservations at first glance, we will introduce some aspects of the anthroposophic view of elemental forces here because of the spiritual insight into the trauma process this view provides.

> As we look out into the world, hosts of elementals who were, or are, continually being enchanted in the processes of densification continually enter into us from our surroundings....Throughout earthly life, elemental beings stream into us. If we only stare at the things that hold elemental beings, these beings simply enter into us untransformed; if we try to work on things in the outer world through ideas, concepts, and feelings of beauty, we redeem and free these spiritual, elemental beings. (Steiner, 2008, CW 110; 23)

When we die it becomes apparent whether we "recognized" and "acknowledged" these beings in our nature observation or whether we walked through nature "blind" and without interest. Elemental beings that have been recognized are redeemed through our insight and set free from their tasks, while those who were ignored remain tied to us and, when we descend to a new incarnation, they are absorbed into our life body from the ether world that borders the physical world. They then live in our life or ether body as a foreign substance that we experience as oppressive and burdensome. "After having passed through life in the spiritual worlds and returning through the gate of birth into the subsequent incarnation, we are accompanied into physical existence by all the elemental beings that were not released. The elemental beings that have been released no longer accompany us, but return to their original element" (Ibid., 45).

Such unredeemed elemental beings will hinder our experience of nature. They may even cause us to be afraid of nature. They hinder the advancement of human thinking.

The second group of **nature beings** is active in the **rhythm of day and night**. According to Rudolf Steiner we redeem these beings by being industrious, while we fetter them to us by being unproductive and lazy.

> When we are apathetic and lazy and let ourselves go, we affect those elemental beings quite differently than we do in being creative, active, diligent, and productive. When we are lazy we become united with certain kinds of elemental beings; the same happens when we are active. (Ibid., 47)

These elemental beings, if they remain unredeemed, we also have to carry with us again in our life body to our next incarnation. "[The elemental beings] we allow to flow into us through the mere illusion of the senses, through laziness and apathy...will be reborn with us in our next incarnation" (Ibid., 47). Such unreleased nature beings that we absorb and that are active in the rhythm of day and night will engender laziness and feelings of aversion in our next incarnation. They paralyze our will.

The third group of **elemental beings** is active in the rhythm of the waxing and waning moon. Cheerfulness, contentedness, and inner peace are the main qualities we need to set these beings free. If we give in to moods of unhappiness and discontent we will tie these beings to us for the next incarnation when they will engender a disposition for discontent and ill temper in our soul.

> Through a harmonious perception of the world, through inner contentment with the world, we free spiritual elemental beings. Through moroseness, ill humor, and discontentment, we imprison elemental beings who would be freed through serenity. Our moods are not only of significance to ourselves—a cheerful or morose attitude can bring about forces of liberation or of imprisonment that flow out from our being.... Thus we have a third kind of elemental spirits, spirits which either are freed at the time of our death or which must enter the world again with us." (Ibid., 48 f.)

These nature beings will, if unredeemed, hinder the advancement of our feeling life.

The fourth group of elemental beings is connected with the **cycle of the year**, the **yearly rhythm** of the sun:

> There is, finally, a fourth kind of elemental being. These activate the course of the sun during the year and participate in bringing about the wakening, fruitful activity of the sun during the summer so that the ripening that occurs from spring to autumn can happen. (Ibid., 49)

We can release this fourth group of nature beings when we cultivate a religious experience of the yearly cycle and the processes of nature. "Such a person does not merely possess an external religiosity but a religious understanding of the processes in nature, and of the spirit that dwells in nature. By means of this kind of devotion such a person is able to liberate elementals of the fourth class that continually stream in and out of the human being and are connected with the course of the sun" (Ibid., 50).

If we look at nature and the rhythms of the year in a materialistic, uninspired way we will bind the elementals of this fourth group to us:

> A person not endowed with this kind of devotion, one who denies or does not perceive the spirit is caught up by our materialistic chaos, is entered by elementals of this fourth class who stream into the person, remaining as they are. At one's death these elementals are either released, or chained so that they must reappear in the world at one's rebirth. (Ibid., 50)

In a future incarnation this will result "in our incapacity to experience religious feelings; in hatred toward everything spiritual, in aggressive materialism" (Lievegoed, 2002, 121f.). The nature beings of the sun cycle will hinder the advancement of our "I" in a future incarnation.

Perpetrator Introjects Can Be Elemental Beings

Such etheric-astral structures in our soul life are real beings. Thoughts, feelings, and will impulses also become beings beyond the threshold to the spiritual world: "These entities are very real" (Steiner, 1997, CW 147, 117). Upon crossing the threshold we encounter elemental etheric-astral beings that we have created through our thinking, feeling, and doing.

> The moment we think a thought we create something astral-etheric, an elemental being that will live as long as the thought exists. It will then dissolve but its "reflection" lingers and is imprinted on the mirror of memory (which actually means "on the surface of our inner organs"). When we call up old thoughts or ideas from memory, we "scan" their structure on the memory-mirror, but we

have to think them again, which means that we have to create those astral-etheric beings anew. (Lievegoed, 2002, 219)

In his lecture course *Education for Special Needs* (1995, CW 317), Steiner describes the surface of our organs, especially that of the brain, as memory mirrors. When we remember past ideas we scan the structure of the astral-etheric creations on the memory-mirror, but we still have to think the original idea again, which means that we have to recreate the same elemental being.

Our normal way of forming **ideas** and of thinking can be disturbed through trauma or other pathological developments. If etheric rhythms and processes are disturbed, as happens in trauma, for instance, we will, in the long term, experience changes to our organs. Our ideas and thoughts will not remain impressions in the memory-mirrors on the surface of our organs, and the corresponding astral-etheric elemental beings will not dissolve but live on. They live on in our organs with a virulence that subconsciously disturbs our lives. "The memory creations don't appear as a 'resting' memory image, but as ideas that develop an active life in the unconscious realm of the organs" (Lievegoed, 2002, 219).

Similar processes occur in our **feeling life**. Through trauma or other psychopathological developments "certain feelings [can] split off and form separate 'islands' that, demon-like, harass our soul life" (Ibid., 220). These "islands" are elemental beings that we ourselves have created in our feeling life.

Our actions can also be affected by such separations and islands when our will impulses are detached from their meaningful context. They establish themselves in the metabolism/limbs system where they develop, subconsciously, a disturbing and destructive life of their own, usually of a compulsive nature. These are elemental beings that we have created in our will life and through our actions.

These subconscious forces are increasingly rising to consciousness today. Depth psychology investigates these "complexes" but fails to recognize their suprasensory dimension. Through extreme stress and trauma these creations of our own life of thinking, feeling, and will may even appear as the "three beasts from the abyss."

In the trauma process these etheric-astral beings, which have been created by the perpetrator's thinking, feeling, and will, may be projected on the victim. As a result the aggressor feels unburdened for a short time. But in the inner organization of the victim these projections unfold their harassing, obstructing, and damaging effect as perpetrator introjects.

Unredeemed Elemental Beings and the Shadow Being

The unredeemed etheric-astral nature beings, which are fettered to our inner life and unfold their disturbing activity there, are imperfections that we cannot, initially, overcome. They are part of our Shadow Being.

> It is an aspect of our double; the clouds of unredeemed elemental beings that hinder us, press heavily on our soul, and make us feel depressed. While the released elemental beings help us further our capacities of spiritual thinking, feeling, and will, the unredeemed elementals form, as a whole, an etheric being that, in certain circumstances, can become detached from us and that we then experience as threatening even though it is tied to us. (Lievegoed, 2002, 122)

Such "certain circumstances" can arise in the aftermath of a traumatic shock. Victims generally respond with memory problems, negativity, lack of interest, inactivity and a frozen will. Trauma can hinder the advancement of our thinking, feeling, and will and of our "I"-development. The ether body becomes detached from the physical body, as do the unredeemed nature beings. More or less consciously, we experience our double as a threat. We meet our own shadow.

Traumatic Influences from Earlier Lives

Over a period of fifteen years, the Rabbi and Chasidic storyteller Yonassan Gershom collected hundreds of moving reports from

Americans who had come to him with a sensitive problem; although they were all born after 1945 they experienced memories of themselves as Jews in Nazi Germany (Gershom, 1977):

> Mary is from the American mid-west. Even as a child she suffered from nightmares of bomb attacks that drove her into a panic. Walking home from school, she often had visions of endless marches. In 1969, when she was 25, she went to visit Germany with her boyfriend. As they boarded a train in Heidelberg and the sliding doors shut Mary suddenly panicked. She gasped and screamed. Memory images rose up in her of freight waggons overcrowded with people being taken to a concentration camp. Mary was convinced: "I was here before, this is where I died!" (Ibid., 125).

> Donnie Ducharme is from Raleigh in North Carolina: "I was born in June 1948 into a Baptist family.... Even when very little I froze with terror at the sight of black boots.... My granddad had gumboots that really scared me. My mother used to put them in front of the stove so I wouldn't go too close and get burned. The boots made sure I always steered clear of the stove. I still see myself walking with my back close to the wall to be as far away from those boots as possible. I didn't understand why I was so scared of those boots until I saw a film about Hitler, with soldiers goose-stepping in front of him. There were the boots! I suddenly had a strong feeling that I had experienced this myself" (Ibid., 126).

According to Steiner's spiritual scientific research the experiences Gershom recounts don't necessarily have to be the memories of the individual in question. Neither are they proof of the continued existence of an individuality through repeated incarnations. They could still be spiritual realities or objective memories, based on the communication between incarnating individualities and the recently deceased. Yet, even if one doubts that the oppressing experiences Gershom describes are evoked by memories of a previous incarnation, the phenomena, if looked at from a spiritual point of view, still pose the question as to whether unresolved experiences from a previous life can cause traumatization in the present incarnation?

Unresolved experiences from previous lives do indeed encroach on our present life. When we die, our "earthly body" (physical body) is left behind in the physical world as a corpse which soon loses its form and dissolves into the elements of the earth. Our spirit-soul first lives on in the ether body, the carrier of our memories. Therefore, in the moment of death when the ether body leaves the physical body we have a panoramic view of our past life. After around three days the ether body becomes an etheric corpse and dissolves into the ether world. Then the astral body dissolves in the astral world. The spiritual dimension, the "I," alone returns to the spiritual world.

Just as there are human-made, artificial substances on earth that do not dissolve and are like foreign substances to the earth organism, there are also insoluble foreign substances produced by human beings that cannot be absorbed by the ether and astral worlds and remain connected with the individuality that created them. Materialistic thinking, feeling, and acting patterns are foreign bodies in the supra-sensory worlds in the same way synthetic materials that do not decompose cannot be integrated in the physical world.

When we descend toward a new birth, these foreign elements that have an affinity with us as their creators, become integrated, as islands, in the newly forming astral and ether bodies. There, they act as disturbing, separate "enclaves" and exert, as impulses, feelings, and thoughts, a negative influence on our lives.

Steiner referred to the etheric encapsulations of unresolved etheric creations as "phantoms" and to their astral counterparts as "demons." Sigmund Freud called them "complexes." They can be like malignant pathological predispositions that haunt and destroy us. C. G. Jung spoke of "possession" in this context.

There are exceptional cases, according to Rudolf Steiner, of an individuality reincarnating before the astral corpse of their former life has entirely dissolved into the astral world. Such "remains" also have something "demonic." They can cause considerable psychic disorders and evoke feelings of guilt that massively interfere with and distort a person's thinking and judgment. This happens in the case of trauma, for instance.

Collective Threshold Experiences

"Yesterday we stood at the precipice. Today we're a step further." This adage, coined by the alternative youth movement, could be read not so many years ago as graffiti on houses that were occupied by squatters. It uses as its motif the standing at the abyss and the crossing of the threshold not of a single person but of humankind as a whole. The collective crossing of the threshold evokes, more or less consciously, experiences comparable to those that individuals have when crossing the threshold—whether they do so consciously as part of a path of inner development or in the moment of death, or unconsciously, during sleep or as a result of illness or trauma. The adage and the experiences underlying it express the mood of an entire generation.

Steiner pointed out that, unconsciously, humankind had collectively crossed the threshold as part of its evolution in the nineteenth century:

> Individual human beings increasingly move on from instinctive, naïve to conscious soul experiences. But for humanity as a whole an important development occurs unconsciously, that individuals are not necessarily aware of.... The foundations of our present historical events are comparable with the experience that individual human beings can only consciously have if they cross the threshold of the spiritual world.... Humanity as a whole is experiencing something similar in our age, as a natural process, as a cosmic, historic event.... Humanity as a whole is crossing the threshold. (Steiner, 1964, CW 192, 62ff.)

Because of this, experiences from beyond the threshold increasingly burst into the soul life of people who are not prepared for them. They are not usually experienced consciously but rather in a dreamlike way and rumble about in the subconscious, erupting here and there and manifesting symptomatically in the disaster scenarios of our time.

The fact that humanity's crossing of the threshold has so far been consciously registered by only a few individuals and has remained largely subconscious, does not mean that the process itself and its effects are not real. Most processes that go on in our organism or environment are not consciously registered and we still do not deny their reality and effects. The same applies to the interaction and mutual influences between us and our environment that are mostly subconscious, too.

> But even if not a single person would notice that this crossing of the threshold by all of humanity is taking place, that humanity in truth is already in the middle of this crossing, the significance of this crossing for the evolution of humankind would still be real. The significance of such an event in the evolution of humanity does not depend on whether it goes unnoticed or not. People can lose their ability to notice things.... But that does not alter the fact that the significance of this event comes to expression in the whole of human evolution. (Steiner, 1980, CW 190, 147)

In collectively crossing the threshold humanity as a whole is standing at the abyss. The often disastrous conditions of our time are a reflection of subconscious, unresolved threshold experiences. In the subconscious regions of the soul, processes are experienced collectively that correspond to those of individuals crossing the threshold; the members of the human organization are loosened collectively; collectively, the soul forces of thinking, feeling, and will are drifting apart, and collective encounters with the double and the guardian are taking place.

According to psychoanalytic models, complexes arise due to problems and developmental tasks that have been repressed and remain in the subconscious. From there they, subliminally, affect, oppress and obstruct our lives and cause mental and physical illnesses. With the help of a therapist, one then tries to lift into consciousness what has been repressed in order to resolve and integrate it into one's biography. Conscious knowledge can heal and set free. In a similar way, the processes and experiences of humanity's collective crossing of the threshold need to be made conscious and resolved so they can be integrated into the collective biography, or history, of humankind. At this level too knowledge is healing and liberating. Knowledge of the threshold situation would make the otherwise necessary projection of unconscious and unresolved experiences onto current events and developments redundant. The abysses of our time, which are often like nightmares, have to do with unconscious and unresolved experiences resulting from humanity's collective crossing of the threshold. There is a simple and effective way of freeing ourselves from these nightmares; we must wake up!

Natural and Accidental Disasters

Earthquakes in China, Peru, and Haiti; tsunamis in Thailand, Indonesia and Japan; landslides in Brazil and on the Philippines; plane crashes, shipping disasters; nuclear disasters; traffic accidents; train derailments; and explosions; natural disasters and accidents have claimed millions of human lives in recent years, left destruction of apocalyptic dimensions, and brought horrendous suffering to people, leaving them severely traumatized. Natural and accidental disasters are not intended, planned, or targeted events. While the victims of such disasters suffer immensely personally, their fundamental trust tends to be not as profoundly shaken as that of people who suffer individual violence, especially at the hand of a close relative. Trauma caused by natural or accidental disasters is therefore less complex and can, as a rule, be more easily resolved (Fischer, 2006, 105).

Natural or accidental disasters don't involve intentions to harm or guilt. Nobody can be blamed directly for the suffering caused by earthquakes, tsunamis, or volcanic eruptions. They are strokes of fate or instances of human failure or "force majeure." There is a spiritual background to natural and accidental disasters, for they are inextricably connected with human morality. The traumatization of individuals due to external devastation has deeper underlying causes that have to do with individual people or groups of people.

Steiner gave a series of lectures in Dornach between June 27 and 29, 1924, explaining the causes and effects of natural and accidental disasters with regard to the victims in question, based on the spiritual view of reincarnation and destiny (karma) (Steiner, 1973, CW 236, 270ff.).

Natural Disasters Have to Do with Old Karma

When we incarnate into a new life we bring prenatal impulses and motives with us that are partially connected with past karma. That is also true of working through natural disasters:

> Up in the spiritual worlds, human souls, in the time between death and a new birth, live in groups based on their karma. They are working out their future karma on the basis of past karmic relationships. And we see how such groups of human souls, in descending from pre-earthly into earthly existence, move toward regions in the vicinity of volcanoes or earthquake-prone areas in order to meet their destiny in such natural disasters. We even find that in this life between death and a new birth, where human souls are guided by entirely different views and sentiments, souls that belong together intentionally seek out such places so they can meet a particular destiny.... "I choose a great disaster so I can become more complete, since otherwise I would not be able to fulfill the karma of my past" (Ibid., 271f.).

Natural disasters such as earthquakes, floods, volcanic eruptions, or hurricanes usually affect the people who live in a particular region and who have, according to Steiner, a karmic relationship:

> When people perish together in an earthquake...they are usually somehow connected by karma—just as people, who live in the same region, usually have a karmic relationship or have something to do with one another. They share a destiny because they have descended to this particular place on earth from their pre-earthly existence and go together toward an event that will sever the threads of their lives. (Ibid., 291)

People who die suddenly in a natural disaster will cross the threshold of death in a different way from people who die naturally as a result of physical degradation. They carry different forces with them across the threshold to the spiritual world.

> This gradual decline...happens in a moment. The physical body can cope with this, but not the etheric and astral bodies or the "I." We will enter the spiritual world differently from the way we would have done if we had completed this life. We carry something into the spiritual world that would otherwise not be there—an etheric body, an astral body and an "I" that might still be living on earth.... They are destined for life on earth, but they are carried into the spiritual world. After each such natural disaster we see how earthly elements are carried into the spiritual world. (Ibid., 294)

"Unused karmic causes" from earlier earthly lives are being carried back across the threshold of death into the spiritual world and will affect the next incarnation of the individuals in question: "There is something that has not taken effect, causes that have not been used. The gods can take these unused causes and bestow them on the individuality, giving them more inner strength for their next incarnation. The causes that were at work behind the earlier incarnation can, as a result, work even more powerfully in the next incarnation. The individual who had not experienced the catastrophe might have been less gifted in life and will return, endowed with particular faculties. One's astral body is condensed because unused karmic causes have been integrated into it" (Ibid., 295f.).

Accidental Disasters Generate New Karma

Karma works in quite a different way in the case of accidental disasters such as a railway accident. The individuals who experience the accident together and, in the worst case, are killed together had no previous karmic relationship but will be karmically connected in their future incarnation because they have shared this experience:

Now think of the difference between such a natural disaster and an event that is entirely due to civilization, like a major railway accident, for instance.... As a rule not many victims of such an accident are karmically connected. Who are the people who find themselves together on such a train? They are not bound by the same ties as the victims of an earthquake. One could say that destiny brings the victims of a railway accident together in one place. (Ibid., 291)

Natural and Accidental Disasters Have Different Karmic Consequences

Natural as well as accidental disasters have the effect on their victims of their astral body being more condensed in the next incarnation, but the consequences will be quite different depending on whether people lost their lives in the one or the other. The victims of natural catastrophes have enhanced karmic memories: "A natural disaster will cause its victims to have an enhanced memory, a clear remembrance, of anything to do with their karma" (Ibid., 296).

With accidental disasters the opposite happens. The astral bodies will be more condensed but, as a consequence, the victims tend to forget the karmic causes in their next incarnation. "A railroad accident or any other human-made disaster causes oblivion with regard to karma.... However, because of this forgetting, the individuals in question grow particularly sensitive to the impressions they receive in the spiritual world after death" (Ibid., 197).

Natural and accidental disasters also have very different consequences for the future make-up of the victims' soul forces in the next incarnation: "Whereas in the case of a natural disaster the victims' intellectual qualities are particularly enhanced, it is the will that is enhanced in victims of accidental disasters. This is how karma works" (Ibid., 197).

Emergency Education as Threshold Education

THE INCIDENCE OF DISASTERS IS INCREASING

Natural disasters have a spiritual background. There is a connection between natural disasters and our soul life.

The folktale of "The Fisherman and his Wife" by the Brothers Grimm (2006) describes in images how our inner life hangs together with the earth's ecology.

> There once was a fisherman and his wife. They lived together in a hovel by the sea. Every day the fisherman went out and he fished and he fished" (Ibid., 59). One day he caught a large flounder who claimed to be an enchanted prince. The fisherman let it go free. When he told his wife she complained that he could have asked the flounder for a house in return for setting it free. She sends her husband back to the sea again to make his wish. "When he got to the sea, it was all green and yellow and no longer transparent" (Ibid., 60).
>
> He called to the fish and told him what his wife wanted and the flounder granted her wish. But his wife was not content. A few weeks later she sent him back to the shore telling him to ask for a castle instead of the house. "When he came to the sea, the water was all violet and dark blue and grey and no longer green and yellow, but it was still calm" (Ibid., 61). He called the fish who granted his wish again. But his wife was still not content; she wished to be queen in her castle. So she sent her husband out again. "And when he came to the sea, the sea was all black-grey, the water heaved up from below and smelled all putrid" (Ibid., 62). Sometime after this wish too had been granted, the fisherman's wife began to yearn for more power. She wished to be empress. So she sent her husband out to ask the fish to grant her wish. Very reluctantly, the fisherman went on his way. "Then the sea was all black and thick and began to foam from the depths so that it threw up bubbles. And a whirlwind swept over the sea so that its surface curled up" (Ibid., 63).
>
> Once the fisherman's wife was empress she desired to be pope. Again, she sent her husband to the sea. "And a high wind blew over the land and the clouds flew, and all grew dark as if night was falling. The leaves fell from the trees, and the water rose and roared as if it were boiling and stormed upon the shore, and in the distance he saw ships which were firing guns in their sore need, pitching and tossing on the waves. And yet in the midst of the sky

there was still a small bit of blue, though on every side it was as red as in a heavy storm" (Ibid., 64). This wish was also granted. But the woman's greed was still not satisfied. She wanted to be like God. "A dreadful storm arose so that he could hardly withstand it. The houses and trees were blown over, and the mountains shook, and rocks rolled into the sea and the heavens became pitch black and lightning played, and the thunders rolled; and the sea rose up in black waves as high as church towers and mountains with crowns of white foam upon their heads" (Ibid., 66). When the fisherman had told the fish about his wife's request, the fish sent him back home: "'Go back home. She is back in her hovel.' And there they still sit to this day" (Ibid., 66).

Modern medicine increasingly acknowledges the psychosomatic background of organic illness. Intrapsychic events such as long-term stress affect the life processes of our organism and can make us ill. The earth can equally be seen as a living organism with a physical, a biological, a psychic and a spiritual dimension, dimensions that are visible in the mineral world, the plant world, the animal world, and in the human world respectively.

Ecological disasters are ultimately caused by our inner attitude as human beings. Unbridled greed in our soul life will manifest in our economic and societal structures that have the potential to destroy the conditions for life on earth. Air pollution, dying trees, climate change, water pollution, the extinction of animal and plant species, or the contamination of entire regions; all these destructive developments have to do with exploitative thinking and economic profit seeking. Inner attitudes can cause natural disasters. We can speak of psychosomatic illnesses here too, but on a global level.

The folktale of the fisherman and his wife describes this circumstance in images. While the imagery of folktales is very complex and defies one-dimensional interpretations, some of the elements in this folktale and its overall message illuminate the link between the human soul life and natural disasters (Geiger, 1998; Lenz, 1997).

Emergency Education as Threshold Education

The folktale is set in the dual world of land and sea, with the land representing the physical sensory world. The sea, which can be interpreted as an elemental soul world with its emotional ups and downs, represents the transition between the physical, sensory and the spiritual, suprasensory worlds. The fish lives in this soul world. It is a creature with no warm blood of its own and can be seen as representing spiritual experiences such as thoughts or inner images. By fishing these out of the sea, we find true nourishment for our souls. Christ's disciples were also fishermen.

We meet this dual world in the characters of the fisherman and his wife who live in a series of changing dwellings. They are the only human beings that appear in the tale. We can look at them as the soul and spirit of the same individual. The fisherman might represent the "I" that is able to delve into the suprasensory soul world where it can find nourishing experiences. His wife could be seen as the soul. The changing dwelling places might stand for the physical body that gives a home to both "I" and soul. In the folktale the fisherman, or the "I," appears to be too weak to control the soul life and, against his will, he becomes the pawn in the hands of uncontrolled soul forces. As a result he causes a disaster of enormous dimensions.

The effects of the global human soul life can manifest locally with catastrophic consequences as floods, droughts, storms, earthquakes, or fires. "The science of initiation can and must ask with regard to elementary events; when was this event prepared? In the horrors and abominations of war and in other aberrations that took place in human evolution" (Steiner 1973, CW 236, 298). The victims of such disasters are not necessarily the same individuals who are directly responsible for them, as Steiner pointed out in various places (Steiner 2001, CW 94; 1964, CW 95; 1989; CW 96; 1975, CW 120; 1973, CW 236).

International rescue activities in the aftermath of natural disasters can consequently be an image of the shared global responsibility we have for such disasters and the suffering of the people involved.

Incidence and intensity of natural disasters have noticeably increased in recent years. The globalization of materialism, greediness, and immorality as well as the lack of a responsible attitude toward life constitute a breeding ground for ecological crises. Just as our organism defends itself when exploited by our soul life, responding with crises, disturbances and illnesses, the life forces of the earth organism respond to being exploited by materialistic lifestyles, greed, and egoism. "Where on the earth will one day erupt with blazing flames or heaving ground what is now burning in the wild passions of human beings" (Steiner 1973, CW 236, 298)? If we look at the state of morality in the world and at the psychosomatic conditions within the earth's organism, we get a sense that the incidence of natural disaster will be increasing.

We Must Expect More Trauma

The concept of "trauma" is widely discussed today. We hear the term used excessively in media reports and ordinary conversations, but also by psychologists and therapists. Almost anything seems to have the potential to cause trauma—murder and manslaughter as much as the defeat of the football club one supports. There are entire regions on earth where the inhabitants are described as "traumatized." According to the United Nations Children's Fund (UNICEF) more than 10 million children are traumatized by war. Countless people are traumatized because they have been displaced, are fleeing, socially excluded, long-term unemployed, and so on. The list is endless. "The boundaries between extreme trauma and the psychic conflicts of everyday life seem to become blurred. Anything is considered to be traumatic today—terror and repression as much as bad grades at school and a lost football match" (Merk and Gebauer, 1997, 2).

Why does trauma seem to be so epidemic today? Are we really exposed to more frequent or more extreme challenges? Previous generations also experienced tremendous natural disasters and wars, crises, personal tragedies, and suffering. Is it not rather a matter of modern trauma research having made us aware and more sensitive toward trauma and its long-term effects?

At the beginning of the last century Steiner revealed that there would be evolutionary changes in the inner human organization as humanity was collectively crossing the threshold and he described the consequences of this development (Steiner, 1983, CW 184). The close ties between physical and life body would grow looser and, as a result, we would experience new soul faculties and forms of consciousness as well as higher degrees of sensitivity.

> We live at a time when the ether body will gradually become more detached from the physical body. This is part of human evolution.... We are in the middle of that process and some of the more subtle symptoms of illness that we experience would be understood if that was known. (Steiner 1982, CW 113, 131f.)

This loosening of the life forces from the physical body will result not only in a widened consciousness and greater sensitivity but also in an increased susceptibility to illness. Because our constitutions are changing, we have become more delicate, more thin-skinned, and therefore more vulnerable. For the same reason we have become more prone to traumatization.

The difference in interplay between the parts of our organization, the loosening of the etheric body from its physical foundation is, anthroposophically speaking, the reason for our increased psychic vulnerability today and the highly increased risk of traumatization. A mere gaze can, today, be enough to injure a child's soul. It might not even need physical violence or a natural disaster to traumatize such delicate children. If we include the spiritual dimension, the process of incarnating into today's materialistic civilization in itself can be a traumatizing experience.

In the lectures he gave in the early twentieth century, Steiner not only pointed out that changes of the human constitution were to be expected, he also described the pedagogical, medical, and therapeutic implication of these evolutionary changes. Waldorf education, an anthroposophically extended medicine, and anthroposophic therapies are practical tools for meeting the changing conditions in the human constitutions.

6

Competence in Stress Management

Emergency Helpers Are under Extreme Stress

Emergency education as crisis intervention is stressful. The members of the intervention teams are often weighed down by an almost unbearable sense of powerlessness. They too come face to face with the inconceivable and experience threshold situations. "*Trauma is contagious*" (Herman, 1994, 193).

The emergency education intervention in Japan was physically and emotionally taxing—not only because of the nuclear disaster in Fukushima. Seeing destruction on such an unimaginable scale is traumatizing in itself even before one has heard the horrifying reports about the disaster. Meeting victims of human-caused suffering, such as massacres, torture, abuse, or rape, where a person's dignity has been brutally injured and their sense of justice perverted or disregarded, is particularly demanding. A married couple whom we spoke to in the Gaza strip showed us a photograph of their three dead children and spoke about their ordeal.

> Our five-year-old was shot in the head. Our nine-month-old baby was also shot. Her eyes were still open in the picture. Our eleven-year-old son was shot twice in the lungs. He kept breathing for two days. We couldn't save him because the soldiers wouldn't let us through to the rescue services.

What these parents described was the execution of their children.

> The stepmother of ten-year-old Abdella is sitting in front of her ruined house in Zeitoun. She is deeply depressed. We give

her beeswax for modelling. She shapes a ball but keeps tearing it apart, sobbing. After some time she is able to talk. She tells us that soldiers have killed her one-year-old daughter. Then she leads us to the place where the crime took place—a room in the destroyed house. On the blood-smeared wall where the dead child lay is written in English: "1 down—999,999 to go" (Melzer, 2010, 299, note 393).

THE LIMITS OF RESILIENCE

The impact of the traumatic experience is reflected in the soul of emergency and trauma teachers. Being able to bear this is one of the competencies emergency helpers need. In working with traumatized children and youngsters we are continuously at risk of reaching the limits of our own ability to withstand stress. The better we know these limits beforehand, the smaller the risk of succumbing to a crisis while we are giving help. The risks of excessive strain or secondary traumatization are often underestimated (Reinhard/Maercker, 2003) and helpers end up overwhelmed by a situation or they begin to show signs of burnout (Reddemann, 2001, 2004).

STRESS FACTORS IN EMERGENCY EDUCATION

Traumatized children and youngsters tend to display difficult and unusual behaviors such as aggression, self-aggression, sexualisation, and loss of trust. They abuse those who are weaker, reject attachment figures, break up relationships and, perpetrators as well as victims, reenact. Educators and therapists often reach the end of their tether when faced with provocative behaviors that leave them feeling helpless and overwhelmed.

> These difficult and unfamiliar behaviors challenge our central values and rules of life. Teachers often fail to see these behaviors as a 'normal reaction to an abnormal childhood.' Instead they experience them as a violation of their pedagogical integrity and personal values.... Aggressive behavior...can provoke aggressive,

sometimes even violent responses from teachers.... Faced with a sense of their own helplessness teachers might, for their own relief, call these youngsters uneducable, impossibly ungrateful and so on. (Weiss, 2006, 143ff)

We cannot ignore the biographical experiences that the children bring with them to the everyday pedagogical situation. Teachers also carry their biographical background into their teaching. These, generally unconscious, biographical motives and experiences can get in the way of finding true understanding for the traumatized children or adolescents. If helpers don't sufficiently reflect on their biographical experiences and motives, there is a possibility "that traumatized girls or boys are used by professional helpers to work through their own trauma" (ibid., 147). Sometimes the wish to help other people is an attempt to heal oneself.

The work with traumatized children and youngsters and their life stories can bring educational attachment figures to the boundaries of their emotional stress tolerance. Their inner trust may be profoundly shaken and their values and beliefs called into question, while they are plagued by emotions and thoughts that are difficult to cope with. "The posttraumatic imagery of traumatized children can evoke intense reactions in the helpers. Some may struggle with feelings of disgust or nausea when confronted with the re-lived misery of flashbacks, the reenactments and stories from children and young people. Supporting trauma victims who suffer from flashbacks is not without its dangers. Teachers may feel powerless as they watch how this state triggers fears, horror and immense suffering in the girls and boys" (ibid., 148f.). All this will not be without its impact on the helpers' own lives. They may develop feelings of guilt, their own sense of safety may be shattered, their joy in life lost. It is therefore mandatory for emergency helpers to work through and resolve existential aspects of their own biographies. "Helpers must be prepared to look after themselves, too" (Mehringer, 1979, 78).

Mental Health and Stress Management

Primary and Secondary Prevention

Mental health is essential to "protect one's soul from acute or chronic stress" (Hausmann, 2005, 150). It is imperative that psychosomatic warning signs are taken seriously and that adequate means are found for dealing with stress so that helpers can renew their resources in good time.

According to Mitchell and Everly (2001, 261ff.) emergency psychology relies on four factors of **primary prevention** that, if they are observed before facing the stressful event, can protect helpers from developing posttraumatic disorders. These factors are information, training, routine, and teamwork.

Secondary prevention is about warding off potential posttraumatic disorders once helpers are facing the stressful situation. Secondary prevention includes talking about stressful experiences, taking breaks and using periods of regeneration between assignments, acquiring distancing and breathing techniques, using visualization and behavior exercises, practicing suitable problem solving strategies, and finding ways of adequately dealing with emotions in stress situations.

Stress Management in the Various Phases of Intervention

During the various phases of their assignment emergency educators are exposed to a variety of stress situations that each holds its own risks and consequences. Stress levels are particularly high in the **acute phase of emergency education interventions.** The chaos one encounters may lead to disorientation, the danger involved may provoke fears, and the lack of information, equipment, and responsibility may leave helpers feeling overwhelmed. Emotional pressure due to shocking experiences can trigger feelings of helplessness and the uncertainty about the outcome of the intervention often leads to helpers feeling depressed (Wothe, 2001, 65).

Professional stress management in acute phases of crisis intervention requires the following competencies (Hausmann, 2006, 151): Helpers must be able to plan their actions so they do not have to act under pressure (take time; first think, then act). Helpers who know their own limitations are not likely to overstep them. Helpers must be able to organize help to make sure they get appropriate breaks.

Early emergency education interventions in the phase when we see posttraumatic stress responses can cause considerable stress for emergency teachers, as they have to deal with suicide threats from victims and possibly with detailed descriptions of what these victims have experienced.

In the phases of **trauma-oriented special and intensive education** the helpers are often confronted with unfamiliar trauma behaviors and details of horrific incidences that will take them to the limits of their own stress resilience.

Emergency education for traumatized children and youngsters **during crisis interventions in war or disaster zones** can also overstretch the helpers' ability to withstand psychological stress (Boscarino et al., 2004). "Conscious and targeted mental health care is crucial in all phases of disaster management. Taking breaks, limiting the intervention times, making sure there is stand-by staff, and conducting team discussions are among the most important strategies" (Hausmann, 2006, 154). Achieving inner closure after an intervention can prove particularly difficult due to lingering impressions, experiences, or reflections. "Symbolic closure is often needed so that helpers can redirect their thoughts and feelings toward their everyday life" (Ibid., 155). If the threatening situation continues, stories of victims who have come through the traumatic event can counter-balance the effects of those stories with a tragic outcome (Rusesabagina, 2005).

> Listening to and passing on such reports can enhance our experience of coherence (awareness of our subjective ability to act), our emotional resilience, and generally our trust that we will be able to cope with future crises, too. Such reports are part

of a remembrance culture that focuses on positive aspects. (Hausmann, 2005, 424)

Basic Personal Competencies in Stress Management

Helpers who are not familiar with trauma theory are particularly susceptible to stress and tend to respond with insecurity and helplessness during emergency education interventions. The extent of their stress tends to make itself felt in resignation, withdrawal, or exclusion. Professional competence, self-reflection, and self-care are fundamental personal skills in working with traumatized children and youngsters (Weiss, 2006, 162ff.).

Know-how and insight form the foundation for managing stressful situations. People who possess the necessary expertise are able to mitigate and limit dangerous and stressful situations. Such **expertise** arises from specific specialist knowledge. Weiss mentions the following skills as part of the basic standards of working with traumatized children or youngsters (ibid., 163)—a basic knowledge of trauma therapy, developmental risks, protection and risk factors, transference and countertransference, attachment theory, as well as the prevention of burnout through self-care.

In addition to gaining factual knowledge, emergency educators need to **practice self-reflection and self-control.** They need to reflect on aspects of their own biography and examine their own values, attachment patterns, and the motives underlying their professional actions. In doing so, they can reveal and reduce subjective distortions of perception, emotion, or interaction. Maintaining self-awareness, self-reflection, and self-control may be tiring and strenuous, but they are vital qualities in teachers who work with traumatized children and youngsters.

Self-care, looking after one's mental health, ultimately constitutes an act of self-preservation in the work with traumatized children and youngsters. It is "possibly the most important skill of the educator.... To avoid vicarious trauma, we can and must protect ourselves; we must be aware of bodily signals, speak about our experiences and feelings, regulate our level of comfort, and learn to be less overwhelmed without becoming defensive" (Weiss, 2006, 168f.).

Institutional Parameters

Institutional parameters for professional stress management are as important for our mental health as the required personal skills. They include preparation (basic and further training), teamwork, and aftercare (evaluation, supervision).

Working with traumatized children and youngsters requires the **specialist training** that conveys the necessary basic knowledge needed to acquire the relevant expertise to deal with trauma-induced behaviors.

However, the training does not end with the gaining of a qualification. "In order to develop a professional identity we need professional experience, we need to witness successful as well as failing processes, and reflect on our work in supervision and collegial reviews" (ibid., 172). The rapid progress of research necessitates continuous further training and the willingness to be lifelong learners.

The **implementation phase** of emergency education, especially in foreign war and disaster zones, involves immense psychological stress and constitutes a major challenge for entire teams of helpers as well as for the individual team members. "Good teams can limit potential specific stresses. This needs a team culture, however, where people can speak about the strains and difficulties of their everyday teaching life. Being able to trustfully share one's experiences with colleagues helps prevent burnout...and is therefore a desirable goal of team culture" (ibid., 174). Building up good collegial teamwork needs time. Working in an **interdisciplinary team** of special teachers, social youth workers, psychologists, physicians, and therapists means that a range of approaches to working with traumatized children and youngsters can be brought together.

Action plans must include preparation as well as review meetings. They must provide a rhythmic structure to the day, with rituals, sufficient resting and relaxation periods, as well as a diet that is as balanced as possible. Changing one's clothes after work can be a symbolic act that helps team members to maintain an inner distance from the events.

Aftercare is another very important factor after stressful emergency assignments. Karutz and Lagossa (2008, 97f.) distinguish between individual-informal and institutional-organized aftercare. Individual aftercare helps team members to structure and integrate experiences into their biography, for instance by talking about them informally with family and friends. In the case of institutional-organized aftercare, this process of assimilation takes place under supervision in a structured setting.

Tapping into Creative-Vitalizing Sources through Inner Development

Stress management has been an integral part of Waldorf education right from its inception. "Then there is something that is easier said than done but constitutes a golden rule for all teachers. Teachers must never become dry or turn sour but strive to remain inwardly fresh and alive" (Steiner, 1974, CW 294, 194). Especially in a school that focuses more than any other educational system on the teacher-child relationship, the teacher's inner attitude becomes one of the main factors of a quality education. Steiner gave a great number of seminars and training courses on how teachers can tap into creative life-bringing sources through inner work and self-education.

Waldorf education offers its own special methods for stress management and the prevention of burnout. These methods are based on special exercises that help teachers find access to an inner source of creative and vitalizing powers. The process of working with these exercises is referred to as "the inner development of the teacher" (Smit, 1989, 9). There are further dimensions to this path, including the meditation on the basic anthroposophic insights into human nature as a means of gaining access to intuitive inspirations for the teaching practice. This is not the place to present the anthroposophic path of inner development in detail, but there is a wealth of literature available on the theme (Steiner, 1992, CW 10; Schiller 1979; Lievegoed, 2002; Smit, 1989; and much more). We will restrict ourselves here to a few paragraphs that deal with such aspects of inner development as are relevant in the context of emergency education and mental health.

Bodily health preserves the instrument we need for working: Anthroposophy sees the physical body as the tool of our spiritual individuality. We cannot achieve anything on earth without our physical body. We are therefore responsible for looking after this instrument by providing body hygiene, nourishment, exercise, sleep, and so on, obviously without becoming obsessed with our own health issues. Our body and soul are both involved in our daily lives. There are times when we are forced to neglect our health in order to meet the daily challenges. Anything that has the potential to make us ill in such a situation should be counterbalanced by positive experiences (Steiner, 1992, CW 10).

Rhythm enlivens: Rhythm and time are inseparably linked with life. There is no life without rhythm. Rhythm provides balance and strength. When our rhythms are upset we lose this balance and become ill in body and soul.

Rhythm is enormously important for our physical health and our sense of being, also in a social context. By bringing rhythm to our everyday life we can uncover vitalizing inner sources of strength. Rhythm is an essential part of making conscious life choices and an important basis for stress management.

Artistic activity awakens creativity: For us to be mentally healthy our soul forces must interact in a harmonious way. This harmony is also the foundation for creative activities such as eurythmy, music, speech, and working with color or form. We absorb and experience art through our feeling. Artistic exercise serves the cultivation of such artistic experiences and it fosters our senses and motor skills.

Whenever we are carrying out artistic activities we become inwardly involved. Creative imagination is rooted in the depths of the human soul and is awakened when we show interest in the world and when we are involved in an artistic activity. "The soul forces of thinking, feeling and will are brought to harmonious interaction when we perceive the potential future form, penetrate it with feeling and create it with willing hands" (Bühler, 1981, 13). Due to the inner activity evoked by our artistic doing, creative forces are set free that strengthen and enliven us in our everyday lives.

Meditation can mobilize spiritual resources: In his book *How to Know Higher Worlds* (Steiner, 1994, CW 10), Steiner provided exercises and meditations which can enhance the way our "I" interacts with the other levels of our human organization. When we prepare ourselves for trauma management and trauma therapy Steiner's "subsidiary exercises" are particularly useful since they aim at bringing about the harmonization of thinking, feeling, and will. In carrying out these exercises we strengthen our "I" so it can better control our thought processes, feelings, and will impulses and we develop equanimity and positive thinking. Gradually, our "spiritual essence" will emerge as an inner source of strength (Glöckler, 1993, 34). More information about the teacher's path of inner development, including practical exercises, can be found in works by Schiller (1979), Smit (1989), and Zimmermann (1997).

Mental Health: Helping Yourself so You Can Help Others

Mental healthcare not only benefits the health of the helper. It is a necessary requirement for professional competence in working with traumatized children and adolescents. It is no coincidence that flight attendants in their emergency announcements instruct passengers that they should, in case of a sudden drop of cabin pressure, first put on their own oxygen masks and then help children and other people in need put on theirs. Adults need to be stable themselves before they can give help to traumatized children and youngsters.

As emergency helpers we must therefore be aware of our own emotions in stressful situations. We must first find our own center, using tools that help us feel grounded and focused again so that we are really present when a child needs our help. Our own calmness will be transmitted to the child. We help trauma victims release any excess energy created by the traumatic shock by speaking to them calmly and in a quiet voice and by adopting reassuring body language, etc. (Levine and Kline, 2008, 39). Helpers need to be stable, centered, and calm. If we look after our own mental health we help ourselves to help others.

7

Crises Can Be Opportunities

Posttraumatic Growth

Just as our physical organism can grow stronger through overcoming an illness, we can grow inwardly by mastering crisis situations. Each developmental threshold in our biography is a moment of crisis which, if we manage to overcome it, can help us mature. Many people who have successfully resolved traumatic experiences speak of their "true inner growth" (Hausmann, 2006, 156) and if we look at our own biography we might find that the life crises and strokes of fate we have been through helped us grow. The Chinese character for "crisis" has two meanings; it can stand for "danger" or "opportunity."

For a long time trauma research concentrated almost exclusively on the psychopathological effects of extreme stress, but more recently the positive effects trauma can have once it has been successfully resolved, have moved into the focus of scientific inquiry (Tedeschi, Park, and Calhoun, 1998). A "Posttraumatic Growth Inventory," containing 21 questions on various areas of life, has been developed to assess posttraumatic growth (Tedeschi and Park, 1996), but, unfortunately, the study results available so far relate only to adults—holocaust survivors, victims of natural disasters, former cancer patients, survivors of myocardial infarction, and rape victims. But while the same scientific evidence is not yet available to us for children and adolescents, clinical experience suggests "that positive effects have been observed also in children who successfully processed traumatic experiences" (Landolt, 2004, 106).

Initial scientific studies have revealed "that threatening events do not only result in an increased risk of psychological disorders, but offer victims the opportunity for personal development and inner growth" (Ibid., 104). This means that trauma can change lives also in positive ways. "Real posttraumatic growth can mean that the relationship we have with our self, with others and with the world and life in general changes" (Hausmann, 2006, 156).

The following positive biographical effects of resolved trauma relate to *"five dimensions of posttraumatic growth"* (Landolt, 2004, 104f.)—human relationships, outlook on life, personal growth, religion, and spirituality, and the validation of one's own life. We have added one entry taken from the "Posttraumatic Growth Inventory" for each of the five dimensions:

1. **Deepened relationships:** "I know now that I can count on other people in times of need." We often observe that relationships, especially within a family but also beyond, improve once a trauma has been successfully resolved. People communicate more openly and find it easier to establish relationships. Their sensitivity toward others has become enhanced. Clinical experience shows that the successful resolution of trauma in children leads to deepened relationships especially with family and friends.

2. **A new outlook on life:** "I gained new interests." People's outlook on life can expand when they have mastered a crisis. They may discover new interests or goals. They take hold of their lives again by setting new goals and developing a new outlook. People foster relationships more than before and deal with time in a different way.

3. **Personal growth:** "I know now that I can cope with challenges." People who have resolved their trauma successfully often gain more trust, self-confidence, maturity and emotional strength. They become stronger individuals. "The knowledge that we

have coped successfully with a challenging situation gives us trust that we will cope with future challenges too. We gain self-confidence" (Landolt, 2004, 105).
4. **Enhanced validation of one's life:** "I think differently now about the priorities in life." After overcoming stress people tend to find it easier to set priorities and differentiate between what is essential and what isn't. They begin to live more consciously and value their life more.
5. **Spiritual-religious deepening:** "I have a better understanding of religious and spiritual things now." People who have come close to death often develop strong spiritual and religious feelings as a result of their extraordinary experience. Trauma can lead people to develop a deeper interest in existential questions and topics.

Helpers who are assigned to war or disaster zones are often confronted with unspeakable suffering, destruction, and despair. But even in the midst of great doom we find examples of spiritual experiences.

> Ernso (27), a teacher from Port au Prince, Haiti, says, "I was in the internet café when the earthquake started, but was able to leave the building. Clouds of dust were all around. People came toward me, covered in blood and screaming. Aimlessly, I walked through town for six hours, trying to find my family and friends. They all survived. Then I fainted, probably because I was so weak. When I came round I remembered that I had dreamt. I had seen my uncle in my dream. He was looking at me imploringly, holding out his arms to me. I ran to my uncle's house. It had collapsed. I began to dig in the ruins and found my uncle alive. He lay there like in my dream, with imploring eyes and his arms stretched out to me."

Helping from a Feeling of Responsibility

Emergency teachers suffer secondary traumatization due to the stress they experience. They often develop symptoms of posttraumatic stress and need to work through their own trauma. They, too, need to transform their crisis into an opportunity for increasing their maturity, for biographical development and posttraumatic growth.

On-going training, professional preparation and debriefing, as well as inner development can help mitigate the traumatic experiences that emergency educators by necessity confront during interventions, so that these experiences can be more easily resolved. These often horrific experiences can be offset by the knowledge that one has, through presence, competence, and pedagogical measures, brought the light back to children's eyes in situations of deepest despair.

Aside from all the devastation and trauma, we hear stories that give us hope and prove that misery can be transformed by actions that grow out of a sense of responsibility. In Ofunato, City Counselor Hirati campaigned for decades for secure stairs to be built from a school, which was situated at a low altitude and therefore not tsunami-proof, to the mountain behind. The city council kept postponing the project for financial reasons. Just before Hirati retired the stairs were built. Shortly after the official inauguration, Hirati died. On Japan's black day all the pupils and teachers of the school were guided to safety along these stairs, before the tsunami tore the building and the stairs away. Hirati's grandchild was among the pupils who were saved.

Bibliography

(entries for Rudolf Steiner listed by "CW" volume number)

Ainsworth, M. et al. (1978): *Patterns of Attachment: A Psychological Study of the Strange Situation*. Hilsdale.

Andreatta, A. (2006): *Die Erschütterung des Weltverständnisses durch Trauma*.

Antonovsky, A. (1997): *Salutogenese. Zur Entmystifizierung der Gesundheit*. Tübingen.

Arbeitsgemeinschaft der Wissenschaftlichen Medizinischen Fachgesellschaften (AWMF): *Leitlinien Psychotherapeutischer Medizin und Psychosomatik: Posttraumatische Belastungsstörung ICD-10: F43.1*. www.uni-duesseldorf.de/AWMF/ll/051-010.htm (30.3.2007).

Auer, W.-M. (2007): *Sinnes-Welten. Die Sinne entwickeln. Wahrnehmung schulen. Mit Freude Lernen*. München.

Barak, M. (2006): *Guidelines for the treatment of mental trauma*. Harduf. (Unveröffentlichtes Manuskript)

Bardt, S. (2010): *Eurythmie als menschenbildende Kraft. Menschenkunde und Erziehung*. Bd. 76. Stuttgart.

Bauer, J. (2006): *Warum ich fühle, was du fühlst. Intuitive Kommunikation und das Geheimnis der Spiegelneuronen*. München.

———. (2009): *Das Gedächtnis des Körpers. Wie Beziehungen und Lebensstile unsere Gene steuern*. Frankfurt.

Baur, A. (1995): *Fliessend Sprechen*. Schaffhausen.

———. (1996): *Die Finger tanzen. Fingerspiele für Kinder von 3 bis 9 Jahren*. Schaffhausen.

Bausum, J.; Besser, L.; Kühn, M.; Weiss, W. (Hrsg.) (2009): *Traumapädagogik. Grundlagen, Arbeitsfelder und Methoden für die pädagogische Praxis*. Weinheim/München.

Besser, L. (2009): Wenn die Vergangenheit die Zukunft bestimmt. Wie Erfahrungen und traumatische Erlebnisse Spuren in unserem Kopf hinterlassen, Gehirn und Persönlichkeit strukturieren und Lebensläufe determinieren. In Bausum, J.; Besser, L.; Kühn, M.; Weiss, W. (2009): *Traumapädagogik. Grundlagen, Arbeitsfelder und Methoden für die pädagogische Praxis*. Weinheim/München. 37–52.

Bijloo, M. (2011): Bindung und Bindungsproblematik. In Niemeijer, M. et al. (2011): *Entwicklungsstörungen bei Kindern und Jugendlichen*.

Medizinisch-pädagogische Begleitung und Behandlung. Stuttgart. 189–205.

Birnthaler, M. (2008): *Erlebnispädagogik und Waldorfpädagogik. Menschenkunde und Erziehung.* 93. Stuttgart.

———. (Hrsg.) (2010): *Praxisbuch Erlebnispädagogik.* Stuttgart.

Blos, K. (2007): Begriff und Ansätze der Psychotherapie. Zum grundlegenden Verständnis ihrer Praxis. In Buchmann, T. (Hrsg.) (2007): *Psychomotorik-Therapie und individuelle Entwicklung. Bewegung bewegt das Denken und Fühlen.* Luzern. 13–15.

Bölt, F. (2005): Junge Menschen stark machen gegen Widrigkeiten und Belastungen. Umgang mit Belastungsstörungen bei Kindern und Jugendlichen in der Schule. In *Pädagogik,* 57. Jg., Heft 4. Hamburg.

Boscarino, J. A. (2004): Posttraumatic stress disorder and physical illness: Results from clinical and epidemiologic studies. *Annals of the New York Academy of Sciences,* 1032, 141–153.

Bowlby, J. (2001): *Verlust, Trauer und Depression.* Frankfurt.

Breiter, R.; Klattenhoff, K. (2005): *Zeiten 4. Deutschland im 20. Jahrhundert. Räume, Zeiten, Gemeinschaften. Unterrichtswerk für den gesellschaftskundlichen Bereich.* Troisdorf.

Brewin, C.; Andrews, B.; Valentine, J. D. (2000): Meta analysis of risk factors for posttraumatic stress disorder in trauma-exposed adults. *Journal of Consulting and Clinical Psychology,* 68. 748ff.

Brinkley, D. and P. Perry (1994). *Saved by the Light: The True Story of a Man Who Died Twice and the Profound Revelations He Received.* New York: HarperCollins, 2008.

Brochmann, I. (1997): *Die Geheimnisse der Kinderzeichnungen. Wie können wir sie verstehen?* Stuttgart.

Brotbeck, K. (1959): *Schiller als Wegbegleiter und Erneuerer unserer Kultur.* Seperatdruck aus «Gegenwart», Nr. 7, Oktober 1959. Bern.

Bub-Jachen, C.-J. (1997): *Schlafstörungen–gesunder Schlaf. Beiträge für eine gesunde Lebensführung in Gesundheit und Krankheit.* Soziale Hygiene 154. Bad Liebenzell.

Buchmann, T. (Hrsg.) (2007): *Psychomotorik-Therapie und individuelle Entwicklung. Bewegung bewegt das Denken und Fühlen.* Luzern.

Buggle, F. (1985): *Die Entwicklungspsychologie Jean Piagets.* Stuttgart.

Bühler, W. (1981): Künstlerisches Tun als Lebenshilfe. In *WELEDA Nachrichten,* Nr. 140, S. 12f. Schwäbisch Gmünd.

Carlgren, F. (1996): *Erziehung zur Freiheit. Die Pädagogik Rudolf Steiners. Menschenkunde und Erziehung.* Bd. 25. Stuttgart.

Compani, M.-L.; Lang, P. (Hrsg.) (2011): *Waldorfkindergarten heute. Eine Einführung.* Stuttgart.

Bibliography

Condon, W. S.; Sander, L. W. (1974): Neonate Movement is synchronized with Adult Speach. Interactional Participation and Language Acquisition. In *Science*, Vol. 183, 11 (1974). 99–101.

Cullberg, J. (1978): *Krisen und Krisentherapie. Psychiatrische Praxis 5.* 25–34.

Dehner-Rau, C.; Reddemann, L. (2008): *Trauma. Folgen erkennen, überwinden und an ihnen wachsen.* Stuttgart.

Denjean-von Stryk, B. (2010): *Sprich, dass ich dich verstehe. Die Sprache als Schulungsweg in Kunst, Erziehung und Therapie.* Stuttgart.

de Raaf, T. (2011): Psychische Gesundheit und Krankheit. In Niemeijer, M. et al. (2011): *Entwicklungsstörungen bei Kindern und Jugendlichen. Medizinisch-pädagogische Begleitung und Behandlung.* Stuttgart. 157–172.

Dietrich, J.; Raschke, F.; Hildebrandt, G. (1982): *The coordination between walking rhythm and heart beat in trained and untrained humans.* Pflügers Archiv 292, R 29.

Ding, U. (2009): Trauma und Schule. Was lässt Peter wieder lernen? Über unsichere Bindungen und sichere Orte in der Schule. In Bausum, J.; Besser, L.; Kühn, M.; Weiss, W. (2009). *Traumapädagogik. Grundlagen, Arbeitsfelder und Methoden für die pädagogische Praxis.* Weinheim/München. 55–66.

Dohm, C. (2002): *Spiel mit mir–Sprich mit mir. Spiele zur Sprachentwicklung vom Kleinkind bis zum Grundschulalter.* Stuttgart.

———. (2009): *Fadenspiele. Mit Freude Hände und Gehirn trainieren.* Stuttgart.

Donowitz, F.; Lache, A. (2011): Verletzte Seele. Wie traumatische Erlebnisse unser Leben beeinträchtigen–und welche Hilfe es gibt. In *Stern.* Nr. 32, 04.08.2011. Hamburg. 68–81.

Dörner, K. (2001): «Ich darf nicht denken». Das medizinische Selbstverständnis der Angeklagten. In Ebbinghaus, A.; Dörner, K. (2001): *Vernichten und Heilen. Der Nürnberger Ärzteprozess und seine Folgen.* Berlin. 331–357.

Dostojewski, F. (1986/1845): *Der Doppelgänger.* Frankfurt.

Eckardt, J. (2005): *Kinder und Trauma.* Göttingen.

Egle, U.; Hoffmann, S.; Joraschky, F. (20053): *Sexueller Missbrauch, Misshandlung, Vernachlässigung.* Stuttgart.

Egloff Lehner, K. (2007): Psychomotorik-Therapie: Balsam für das kindliche Hirn. Motorik, Emotion und Kognition stehen in enger Interaktion. In Buchmann, T. (Hrsg.) (2007): *Psychomotorik-Therapie und individuelle Entwicklung. Bewegung bewegt das Denken und Fühlen.* Luzern. 39–41.

Eissele, I. (2007): *Einfach totgestochen.* www.stern.de. 22.05.2007.

Emmendinger, P. (2010): Klettern–Methoden der Grenzerfahrung. In Birnthaler, M. (Hrsg.) (2010): *Praxisbuch Erlebnispädagogik.* Stuttgart. 54–75.

Endres, M.; Biermann, G. (2002): *Traumatisierung in Kindheit und Jugend.* Munich: Reinhardt Ernst Verlag.

Erikson, E. H. (2000): *Identität und Lebenszyklus.* Frankfurt.

Fietzek, E. (2006): *Das Ungeheuer Trauma. Psychoanalytische Therapie mit seelisch schwer verletzten Menschen.* Frankfurt.

Fingado, Monika (2011). *Rhythmic Einreibung: A Handbook from the Ita Wegman Clinic.* Edinburgh: Floris Books, 2001.

Fischer, G. (2006): *Neue Wege aus dem Trauma. Erste Hilfe bei schweren seelischen Belastungen.* Düsseldorf.

Fischer, G.; Riedesser, P. (1999): *Lehrbuch der Psychotraumatologie.* München.

Frankl, V. (200821): *Der Mensch vor der Frage nach dem Sinn.* München.

Freeman, A.; Dattilio, F. M. (1994): Indroduction to cognitive-behavioral strategies in crisis intervention. In Datillio, F. M.; Freeman, A. (Hrsg.): *Cognitive-Behavioral Strategies in Crisis Intervention.* New York.

Gauda, G. (2008): *Traumatherapie und Puppenspiel. Wie Dornröschen sich selbst erlöste.* Norderstedt.

Gebrüder Grimm (2006): Von dem Fischer un syner Frau. In Gebrüder Grimm (2006): *Kinder- und Hausmärchen. Gesamtausgabe.* Bindlach. 59–66.

Geiger, R. (1998): *Märchenkunde. Mensch und Schicksal im Spiegel der Grimmschen Märchen.* Stuttgart.

Gershom, Y. (1997): *Kehren die Opfer des Holocaust wieder?* Dornach.

Giesen, T. (2011): Unaufmerksamkeit und Hyperaktivität. In Niemeijer, M. et al. (2011): *Entwicklungsstörungen bei Kindern und Jugendlichen. Medizinisch-pädagogische Begleitung und Behandlung.* Stuttgart. 227–245.

Glanzmann, G. (2004): Psychologische Betreuung von Kindern. In Bengel, J. (Hrsg.): *Psychologie in Notfallmedizin und Rettungsdienst.* Berlin. 133ff.

Glas, N. (1975): *Die Hände offenbaren den Menschen.* Stuttgart.

Glöckler, M. (1992): *Begabung und Behinderung. Praktische Hinweise für Erziehungs- und Schicksalsfragen.* Praxis Anthroposophie. Bd. 46. Stuttgart.

———. (1993): Erziehung als therapeutische Aufgabe. In Leber, S. (Hrsg.) (1993): *Waldorfschule heute.* Stuttgart.

———. (1998a): Rudolf Steiner. In Grimm, R. (Hrsg.) (1998a): *Selbstentwicklung des Erziehers in heilpädagogischen Aufgabenfeldern. Die Idee der Selbsterziehung bei H. Nohl, P. Moor, J. Muth, J. Korczak und R. Steiner. Dornacher Reihe.* Bd. 2. Luzern. 53ff.

———. (1998b): *Das Schulkind–Gemeinsame Aufgaben von Arzt und Lehrer. Konstitutionsfragen, Unterrichtsschwierigkeiten, therapeutische Lehrplanprinzipien.* Persephone 2. Dornach/Schweiz.

———. (1998c): *Gesundheit und Schule.* Reihe: Persephone 11. Dornach.

Bibliography

———. (2006): *Kraftquelle Rhythmus.* Anthrosana Nr. 213. Arlesheim.

Glöckler, M.; Denger, J.; Schmidt-Brabant, M. (1993): *Sind wir überfordert? Schulungswege in Heilpädagogik und Sozialtherapie zwischen Selbstfindung und Dienst am anderen.* Persephone 5. Dornach.

Glöckler, M.; Heine, R. (Hrsg.) (2003): *Handeln im Umfeld des Todes.* Persephone, Kongressband Nr. 4. Dornach.

Goebel, W.; Glöckler, M. (2005): *Kindersprechstunde.* Stuttgart.

Grill, H. (2010): *Das Wesensgeheimnis der psychischen Erkrankungen.* Vaihingen/Enz.

Grossmann, K. E.; Grossmann, K. (2003): *Bindung und menschliche Entwicklung.* Stuttgart.

Grözinger, W. (1970): *Kinder kritzeln, zeichnen, malen. Die Frühformen des kindlichen Gestaltens.* München.

Gschwend, G. (2004): *Notfallpsychologie und Traumatherapie. Ein Handbuch für die Praxis.* Bern.

Hagemann, W. (2009): *Burnout bei Lehrern. Ursachen, Hilfen, Therapien.* München.

Hartmann, G. (1971): *Goetheanum Glasfenster.* Dornach.

Hasler, E. (2007): Musik in der Psychotherapie. Beispiele aus der Praxis. In Buchmann, T. (Hrsg.) (2007): *Psychomotorik-Therapie und individuelle Entwicklung. Bewegung bewegt das Denken und Fühlen.* Luzern. 59–61.

Hausmann, C. (2005): *Handbuch Notfallpsychologie und Traumabewältigung. Grundlagen, Interventionen, Versorgungsstandards.* Wien.

———. (2006): *Einführung in die Psychotraumatologie.* Wien.

Herman, J. (1994): *Die Narben der Gewalt. Traumatische Erfahrungen verstehen und überwinden.* Paderborn.

Hermann, I. (2005): Wie kommt Tim denn in den Himmel? Mit Kindern über Sterben und Tod sprechen. *Gesundheit aktiv.* Nr. 184. Bad Liebenzell.

Herzka, H. S. (2007): Bewegungstherapie–ein Zugang zur Zwei-Einheit. In Buchmann, T. (Hrsg.) (2007): *Psychomotorik-Therapie und individuelle Entwicklung. Bewegung bewegt das Denken und Fühlen.* Luzern. 43–44.

Heusser, P.; Selg, P. (2011): *Das Leib-Seele-Problem. Zur Entwicklung eines geistgemässen Menschenbildes in der Medizin des 20. Jahrhunderts.* Arlesheim.

Hilweg, W.; Ullmann, E. (1998): *Kindheit und Trauma. Trennung, Missbrauch, Krieg.* Göttingen.

Herbert, M. (1999): Posttraumatische Belastung. Die Erinnerung an die Katastrophe, und wie Kinder lernen, damit zu leben. Bern.

Howell, E. F. (2002): Back to the "states": Victim and Abuser States in Borderline Personalty Disorder. *Psychoanal Dialog.* 12 (6). 921–957.

Huber, M. (2003a): Trauma und die Folgen. Trauma und Traumabehandlung. Teil 1. Paderborn.

Huber, M. (2003b): Wege der Traumabehandlung. Trauma und Traumabehandlung. Teil 2. Paderborn.

Hüther, G. (2002): Und nichts wird fortan sein wie bisher. Die Folgen traumatischer Kindheitserfahrungen für die weitere Hirnentwicklung. In PAN, Pflege- und Adoptionsfamilien NRW e.V. (Hrsg.): Traumatisierte Kinder in Pflege- und Adoptivfamilien. Ratingen.

———. (2008): *Die Macht der inneren Bilder. Wie Visionen das Gehirn, den Menschen und die Welt verändern*. Göttingen.

Jantzen, W. (2003): Natur, Psyche und Gesellschaft im heilpädagogischen Feld. In *Zeitschrift für Heilpädagogik*, 2/2003. 59ff.

Jenni, O. (2007): Psychomotorik: die Sicht eines Entwicklungspädiaters. Interdisziplinäre Ausrichtung der Psychomotorik und Entwicklungspädiatrie. In Buchmann, T. (Hrsg.) (2007): *Psychomotorik-Therapie und individuelle Entwicklung. Bewegung bewegt das Denken und Fühlen*. Luzern. 31–32.

Juen, B. (2002): *Krisenintervention bei Kindern und Jugendlichen*. Innsbruck.

Jung, C. G. (1967): *Struktur der Seele, Gesammelte Werke*. Bd. 8.

Kaiser, K. (2011): Unvorbereitetes Schwellen-Erlebnis. In *Anthroposophie weltweit*. Nrs. 1–2/11. 3.

Kalmanowitz, D.; Lloyd, B. (o. J.): *Art Therapy and Political Violence*. Routledge. London/New York.

Karutz, H. (2004): *Psychische Erste Hilfe für unverletzte–betroffene Kinder in Notfallsituationen*. Münster.

———. (2011): *Notfallpädagogik. Ideen und Konzepte*. Edewecht.

Karutz, H.; Lagossa, F. (2008): *Kinder in Notfällen. Psychische Erste Hilfe und Nachsorge*. Edewecht.

Kast, V. (2004): *Der Schatten in uns. Die subversive Lebenskraft*. München.

———. (2007): *Die Tiefenpsychologie nach C. G. Jung. Eine praktische Orientierungshilfe. Psychologie konkret*. Stuttgart.

Kayser, M. (1996): Die geistigen Ursprünge der Waldorfpädagogik. In Kayer, M.; Wagemann, P. A. (1996): *Wie frei ist die Waldorfschule. Geschichte und Praxis einer pädagogischen Utopie*. München.

Key, E. (2010): *Das Jahrhundert des Kindes*. Neuenkirchen.

Kiersch, J. (1997): *Die Waldorfpädagogik. Eine Einführung in die Pädagogik Rudolf Steiners*. Stuttgart.

Kissling-Fischer, I. (2007): Bewegung als Auslöser kognitiver, emotionaler und sozialer Prozesse. Psychomotorik–ein Konzept des ganzheitlichen Lernens. In Buchmann, T. (Hrsg.) (2007): *Psychomotorik-Therapie und individuelle Entwicklung. Bewegung bewegt das Denken und Fühlen.* Luzern. 17–19.

Kocija-Hercigonja, D. (1998): Kinder im Krieg. Erfahrungen aus Kroatien. In Hilweg, W.; Ullmann, E. (1998): *Kindheit und Trauma. Trennung, Missbrauch, Krieg.* Göttingen. 177ff.

Köhler, H. (1990): *Jugend im Zwiespalt. Eine Psychologie der Pubertät für Eltern und Erzieher.* Stuttgart.

———. (1994): *Von ängstlichen, traurigen und unruhigen Kindern. Grundlagen einer spirituellen Erziehungspraxis.* Stuttgart.

König, K. (1986): *Kindersprechstunde.* Stuttgart.

Kranich, E. M.; Patzlaff, R.; Schiller, H.; Schuchardt, M. (1992): *Die Bedeutung des Rhythmus in der Erziehung. Beiträge zur Pädagogik Rudolf Steiners 2.* Stuttgart.

Krautkrämer-Oberhoff, M. (2009): Traumapädagogik in der Heimerziehung. Biografiearbeit mit dem Lebensbuch «Meine Geschichte». In Bausum, J.; Besser, L.; Kühn, M.; Weiss, W. (2009): *Traumapädagogik. Grundlagen, Arbeitsfelder und Methoden für die pädagogische Praxis.* Weinheim/ München. 115–126.

Krüger, A. (2007a): *Erste Hilfe für traumatisierte Kinder.* Düsseldorf.

———. (2007b): Psychotrauma bei Kindern und Jugendlichen: Diagnose und Therapie. In *Kindesmisshandlung und -vernachlässigung. Interdisziplinäre Fachzeitschrift der Deutschen Gesellschaft gegen Kindesmisshandlung und -vernachlässigung* (DGgKV) e.V., Jg. 10, Heft 2. 42–64.

———. (2008): *Akute psychische Traumatisierung bei Kindern und Jugendlichen. Ein Manual zur ambulanten Versorgung.* Stuttgart.

Krüger, A.; Reddemann, L. (2007): *Psychodynamisch Imaginative Traumatherapie für Kinder und Jugendliche. PITT-KID. Das Manual.* Stuttgart.

Krüsman, M.; Müller-Cyran, A. (2005): Trauma und frühe Intervention. Möglichkeiten und Grenzen von Krisenintervention und Notfallpsychologie. *Leben lernen 182.* Stuttgart.

Kübler-Ross, E. (1983): *Interviews mit Sterbenden.* Gütersloh.

Kühn, M. (2009): «Macht Eure Welt endlich wieder mit zu meiner!» Anmerkungen zum Begriff der Traumapädagogik. In Bausum, J.; Besser, L.; Kühn, M.; Weiss, W. (2009): *Traumapädagogik. Grundlagen, Arbeitsfelder und Methoden für die pädagogische Praxis.* Weinheim/ München. 23–35.

Kumberger, E. (2007): Trauma im Kindesalter. Traumatische Situationen, Auswirkungen und pädagogische Aspekte. In *Traumapädagogik.*

Heilpädagogische Zugänge zu Menschen mit Traumata. Fachakademie für Heilpädagogik. Regensburg. 27–48.

Labisch, A. (2001): Die «hygienische Revolution» im medizinischen Denken. Medizinisches Wissen und ärztliches Handeln. In Ebbinghaus, A.; Dörner, K. (Hrsg.) (2001): *Vernichten und heilen. Der Nürnberger Ärzteprozess und seine Folgen.* Berlin. 68–89.

Landolt, M. A. (2000): Die Psychologie des verunfallten Kindes. In *Anaesthesiologie, Intensivmedizin, Notfallmedizin, Schmerztherapie.* 35. 615ff.

———. (2003a): Das psychisch traumatisierte Kind. In *Pädiatrische Praxis*, 63. 599ff.

———. (2003b): Die Bewältigung akuter Psychotraumata im Kindesalter. In *Praxis der Kinderpsychologie und Kinderpsychiatrie*, 52. 71ff.

———. (2004): *Psychotraumatologie des Kindesalters.* Göttingen.

Lang, F. (2010): Zirkus–ein Varieté der Möglichkeiten. In Birnthaler, M. (Hrsg.) (2010): *Praxisbuch Erlebnispädagogik.* Stuttgart. 174–203.

Leber, S. (1992): *Die Pädagogik der Waldorfschule und ihre Grundlagen.* Darmstadt.

———. (1993): *Die Menschenkunde der Waldorfpädagogik. Anthropologische Grundlagen der Erziehung des Kindes und Jugendlichen.* Stuttgart.

Leber, S.; Kranich, E. M.; Smit, J.; Zimmermann, H.; Schuberth, E. (1990): *Der Rhythmus von Wachen und Schlafen. Seine Bedeutung im Kindes- und Jugendalter. Studien zur Pädagogik Rudolf Steiners.* Stuttgart.

Lenz, F. (1997): *Bildsprache der Märchen.* Stuttgart. 245ff.

Levi, P. (1993): *Die Untergegangenen und die Geretteten.* München.

Levine, P. A.; Kline, M. (2005): *Verwundete Kinderseelen heilen. Wie Kinder und Jugendliche traumatische Erlebnisse überwinden können.* München.

———. (2006). *Trauma through a Child's Eyes: Awakening the Ordinary Miracle of Healing.* Berkeley, CA: North Atlantic Books, 2007.

———. (2008). *Trauma-Proofing Your Kids: A Parent's Guide for Instilling Confidence, Joy and Resilience.* Berkeley, CA: North Atlantic Books, 2008.

———. (2010): *Kinder vor seelischen Verletzungen schützen. Wie wir sie vor traumatischen Erfahrungen bewahren und im Ernstfall unterstützen können.* München.

Lievegoed, B. C. J. (1979): *Lebenskrisen–Lebenschancen. Die Entwicklung des Menschen zwischen Kindheit und Alter.* München.

———. (1995): *Entwicklungsphasen des Kindes.* Stuttgart (*Phases of Childhood: Growing in Body, Soul and Spirit.* Edinburgh: Floris Books, 2005).

———. (2002): *Der Mensch an der Schwelle. Biographische Krisen und Entwicklungsmöglichkeiten*. Stuttgart (*Man on the Threshold: Challenge of Inner Development*. Stroud, UK: Hawthorn Press, 1990).

Loebell, P. (2011): *Waldorfschule heute. Eine Einführung*. Stuttgart.

Lüpke, H. v. (2000): Identität als wechselseitiger Prozess von Anfang an. In *motorik*, 23 (3). 108–112.

Lutzker, P. (1996): *Der Sprachsinn. Sprachwahrnehmung als Sinnesvorgang*. Stuttgart.

Maercker, A. (1998): Extrembelastungen ohne psychische Folgeschäden: Gesundheitspsychologische Konzepte und Befunde. In Schüffel et al. (Hrsg.): *Handbuch der Salutogenese: Konzept und Praxis*. Wiesbaden. 341–350.

Maercker, A.; Zöllner, T. (2004): The Janus face of self-perceived growth: Toward a two-component model of Posttraumatic Growth. *Psychological Inquiry*, 15. 41–48.

Markowitsch, H. J.; Welzer, H. (2005): *Das autobiographische Gedächtnis. Hirnorganische Grundlagen und biosoziale Entwicklung*. Stuttgart.

Martens, M. G.; Schäfer, S. (2010): *Die verborgenen Wirkungen derSprache im Kindergarten. Anregungen zum spielenden Umgang mit den Sprachkräften*. Stuttgart.

May, A. (2003): *Traumatisierte Kinder. Pädagogische und therapeutische Möglichkeiten der Intervention*. Berlin.

Meck-Bauer, I. (2008): *Biografiearbeit mit psychisch traumatisierten Jugendlichen. Möglichkeiten und Grenzen der Biografiearbeit*. Saarbrücken.

Mehringer, A. (1979): *Eine kleine Heilpädagogik*. München/Basel.

Melzer, A. (Hrsg.) (2010): *Bericht der Untersuchungskommission der Vereinten Nationen über den Gaza-Konflikt*. Rüssingen.

Menasse, R. (2001): *Die Vertreibung aus der Hölle*. Frankfurt.

Merk, U.; Gebauer, T. (1997): *Schnelle Eingreiftruppe «Seele». Auf dem Weg in die therapeutische Weltgesellschaft. Texte für eine kritische Trauma-Arbeit*. Medico Report 20. Frankfurt.

Messner, R. (1987): *Grenzbereich Todeszone*. Köln.

Meyer, U.; Beckmann, W. (2007): Sonderpädagogisches Individualprogramm für nicht schulbesuchsfähige Kinder. In Plume, E.; Adams, G.; Beck, A.; Warnke, A. (Hrsg.) (2007): *Kind und Zeit. Psychische Störungen–Entwicklungsverlauf und gesellschaftlicher Wandel*. Lengerich.

Ministerium für Kultus, Jugend und Sport, Baden-Württemberg (Hrsg.) (2004): *Vom Umgang mit Trauer in der Schule. Handreichungen für Lehrkräfte und Erzieher/innen*. Stuttgart.

Mitchell, J.; Everly, G. (1998): *Stressverarbeitung nach belastenden Ereignissen. Zur Prävention psychischer Traumatisierung.* Edewecht.

———. (2001): *Critical Incident Stress Debriefing.* 3rd rev. ed. Ellicot City: Chevron.

Moody, R. A. (1977): *Leben nach dem Tod. Die Erforschung einer unerklärten Erfahrung.* Hamburg (*Life after Life: The Investigation of a Phenomenon.* New York: HarperCollins, 2001).

Morgan, S. (2007): *Wenn das Unfassbare geschieht–vom Umgang mit seelischen Traumatisierungen.* Stuttgart.

Müller-Wiedemann, H. (1974): Grundlagen einer allgemeinen heilpädagogischen Konstitutionsdiagnostik. In *Beiträge zur heilpädagogischen Methodik.* Stuttgart.

Müller-Wiedemann, H. (1993): Mitte der Kindheit. In Leber, S. (19923): *Die Pädagogik der Waldorfschule und ihre Grundlagen.* Darmstadt.

Neumann, K. D. (1994): Über die Schwelle. Das Lösen des Zusammenhangs von Denken, Fühlen und Wollen. In *Hüter der Schwelle. Der Mensch am Abgrund. Flensburger Hefte.* 45, 6/1994. 35–52.

Niemeijer, M. (2011a): Diagnostik. In Niemeijer, M. et al. (2011): *Entwicklungsstörungen bei Kindern und Jugendlichen. Medizinisch-Pädagogische Begleitung und Behandlung.* Dornach. 77–101.

———. (2011b): Konstitutionsbilder. In Niemeijer, M. et al. (2011): *Entwicklungsstörungen bei Kindern und Jugendlichen. Medizinisch-Pädagogische Begleitung und Behandlung.* Dornach. 103–134.

———. (2011c): Begleiten und Behandeln. In Niemeijer, M. et al. (2011): *Entwicklungsstörungen bei Kindern und Jugendlichen. Medizinisch-Pädagogische Begleitung und Behandlung.* Dornach. 135–153.

Opp, G.; Fingerle, M. (2008): *Was Kinder stark macht. Erziehung zwischen Risiko und Resilienz.* München/Basel.

Oppikofer, R. (2007): Zeichne mir deinen Körper! oder vom Zeichnen in der Psychomotorik. In Buchmann, T. (Hrsg.) (2007): *Psychomotorik-Therapie und individuelle Entwicklung. Bewegung bewegt das Denken und Fühlen.* Luzern. 55–58.

Ott, G.; Proskauer, H. O. (Hrsg.) (1992): *J. W. Goethe: Zur Farbenlehre.* Bd. 5. Stuttgart.

Palm, B. (2010): *Posttraumatischer Stress bei Einsatzkräften: Möglichkeiten und Grenzen der sozialen Arbeit. Erforschung des Arbeitsfeldes «Rescue Social Worker» im Bereich der Notfallpädagogik.* Saarbrücken.

Patzlaff, R. (1999): Kindheit verstummt. Verlust und Pflege der Sprache im Medienzeitalter. In *Erziehungskunst. Monatsschrift zur Pädagogik Rudolf Steiners.* 7/8, Juli/August 1999. Stuttgart. 779–802.

Bibliography

Pearlin, L. (1987): The Stress Process and Strategies of Intervention. In Hurrelmann, K.; Kaufmann, F.; Lösel, F. (Hrsg.) (1987): *Social Intervention: Potential and Constraints*. Berlin.

Pearlin, L.; Mullan, J; Semple, S; Skaff, M. (1990): Caregiving and the stress process: An overview of concepts and their measures. *Geronzology, 45*. 192–199.

Peichl, J. (2007): *Die Inneren Trauma-Landschaften. Borderline, Ego-State, Täter-Introjekt*. Stuttgart.

Perry, B. (2003): Gewalt und Kindheit. Wie ständige Angst das Gehirn eines Kindes im Wachstum beeinflussen kann. In May, A.; Remus, N. (2003): *Traumatisierte Kinder*. Berlin.

Perry, B.; Szalavitz, M. (2009): *Der Junge, der wie ein Hund gehalten wurde. Was traumatisierte Kinder uns über Leid, Liebe und Heilung lehren können*. München.

Pollak, T. (o. J.): *Bis hierher–und weiter? Gedanken über Intensivbetreuung als Chance für nicht gruppenfähige Schüler*. Tübingen.

———. (1998): *Am Rande der Beschulbarkeit. Aussenklasse der Schule für Erziehungshilfe–Konzeption zur Betreuung nicht-gruppenfähiger Jugendlicher*. Tübingen.

Prior, S. (1996): *Object Relations in Severe Trauma*. Northvale, NJ/USA.

Reddemann, L. (2001): *Imagination als heilsame Kraft*. München.

———. (2008): *Psychodynamisch Imaginative Traumatherapie. PITT–das Manual*. München.

———. (2010): *Eine Reise von 1.000 Meilen beginnt mit dem ersten Schritt. Seelische Kräfte entwickeln und fördern*. Freiburg.

Reddemann, L.; Dehner-Rau, C. (2008): *Trauma: Ungelöste Folgen erkennen, überwinden und an ihnen wachsen*. Stuttgart.

Reinhard, F.; Maercker, A. (2003): Sekundäre Traumatisierung, Posttraumatische Belastungsstörung; Burnout und Soziale Unterstützung bei medizinischem Rettungspersonal. *Zeitschrift für Medizinische Psychologie*. 12. 1–8.

Reveriego, M. (2001): Die Parzival Schulen. «Verhaltensgestörte» und «lernbehinderte» Kinder lernen gemeinsam. In *Erziehungs-kunst. Monatsschrift zur Pädagogik Rudolf Steiners*. 65. Jg., 5/Mai 2001. 598–599.

Reveriego, M.; Ruf, B. (2000): «Durchschreite das Tal»—«Mitten hindurch». Parzival-Schulen verwirklichen besonderes Integrationsmodell. In *Karlsruher Kind*. Oktober 2000. 14.

Richard, R.; Krafft-Schöning, B. (2007): *Nur ein Mausklick bis zum Grauen. Jugend und Medien*. Schriftenreihe der Medienanstalt Sachsen-Anhalt. Bd. 7. Berlin.

Ritchie, G. (1995): *Mein Leben nach dem Sterben.* Stuttgart (*My Life after Dying: Becoming Alive to Universal Love.* Charlottesville, VA: Hampton Roads, 1991).

Ritchie, G.; Sherrill, E. (2004): *Rückkehr von morgen.* Marburg (*Return from Tomorrow.* Grand Rapids, MI: Chosen Books, 2007).

Rittelmeyer, C. (1994): *Schulbauten positiv gestalten.* Wiesbaden.

———. (2002): *Pädagogische Anthropologie des Leibes. Biologische Voraussetzungen der Erziehung und Bildung.* Weinheim/München.

———. (2007): *Kindheit in Bedrängnis. Zwischen Kulturindustrie und technokratischer Bildungsreform.* Stuttgart.

Rizzolatti, G. et al. (1996): Premotor cortex and the recognition of motor actions. In *Cognitive Brain Research 3.* 131–141.

Rosslenbroich, B. (1994): *Die rhythmische Organisation des Menschen. Aus der chronobiologischen Forschung.* Stuttgart.

Roszell, C. (1993): *Erlebnisse an der Todesschwelle.* Stuttgart.

Rothschild, B. (2002): *Der Körper erinnert sich. Die Psychophysiologie des Trauma und der Traumabehandlung.* Essen.

Ruf, B. (2008a): Wenn sich das Unbeschreibliche ereignet. Waldorfpädagogik als Notfallpädagogik im Umgang mit psychotraumatisierten Kindern und Jugendlichen. In Schiller, H. (2008): *Wirklichkeit und Idee.* Stuttgart.

———. (2008b): Wenn Welten einstürzen. Notfall-Pädagogik in der Erdbebenregion Sichuan/China. In *Erziehungskunst. Zeitschrift zur Pädagogik Rudolf Steiners.* 72. Jg., 9/September 2008. 979–983.

———. (2009a): Trümmer und Traumata. Krisenintervention in Gaza. In *Erziehungskunst. Zeitschrift zur Pädagogik Rudolf Steiners.* 73. Jg., 3/ März 2009. 297–301.

———. (2009b): In den Köpfen geht das Schiessen weiter. Waldorfpädagogik als Notfallpädagogik mit psychotraumatisierten Kindern im Gaza-Streifen. In *Seelenpflege in Heilpädagogik und Sozialtherapie.* 28. Jg., 2009, H. 4, 6–15.

———. (2009c): Pädagogik in den Ruinen von Gaza. Notfallpädagogik mit kriegstraumatisierten Kindern im Gaza-Streifen. In *Punkt und Kreis.* Weihnachten 2009, H. 18. 8–11.

———. (2010a): Erste Hilfe für die Seele. In *Erziehungskunst. Waldorfpädagogik heute.* 74. Jg., 2/2010. 48–49.

———. (2010b): Verzweifelt, verstört und verlassen. Notfallpädagogischer Einsatz in Haiti. In *Erziehungskunst. Zeitschrift zur Pädagogik Rudolf Steiners.* 74. Jg., 5/Mai 2010. 40f.

———. (2010c): Schutzräume für Kinder. Waldorfpädagogisch orientierte «Child friendly Spaces» für traumatisierte Kinder im vom Erdbeben zerstörten Haiti. In *Die Christengemeinschaft.* 7–8/2010. 405–409.

Bibliography

---. (2010d): Zerstörte Seelenlandschaften. Waldorfpädagogik als Notfallpädagogik für psychotraumatisierte Kinder und Jugendliche. In *Seelenpflege für Heilpädagogik und Sozialtherapie.* 4/2010. Dornach. 45–49.

---. (2011a): Schule als «sicherer Ort». Waldorfpädagogik als Notfallpädagogik im interethnischen Konflikt in Südkirgisistan. In *Freunde der Erziehungskunst Rudolf Steiners (Hrsg.): Rundbrief Sommer 2011.* 34–37.

---. (2011b): Erschütternde Bilder–erschütterte Seelen. Waldorfpädagogik als Notfallpädagogik im nordjapanischen Katastrophengebiet. In *Anthroposophie weltweit.* 6/2011. Stuttgart. 14.

---. (2011c): Erste Hilfe für die Seele. Wie Kinder durch Notfallpädagogik schwere Traumata überwinden lernen. In Neider, A. (2011): *Krisenbewältigung, Widerstandskräfte, Soziale Bedingungen im Kinder- und Jugendalter.* Stuttgart, 173–228.

Rusesabagina, P. (2005): Ein Drink mit den Mördern. Interview mit Kerstin Kohlenberg. *Die Zeit.* 10.2.2005.

Rutishauser Ramm, Beatrice (2011): *Frieden lernen: Friedens- und Notfallpädagogik als Herausforderung in Krisenzeiten.* Basel.

Schad, W. (1979): Die Scham als Entwicklungsraum. In *Die Drei. Zeitschrift für Wissenschaft, Kunst und soziales Leben.* 12/1979. 745–755.

Schefer, J.; Moos, R. (1992): Life crisis and personal growth. In Carpenter, B. (Hrsg.) (1992): *Personal Coping Theory, Research and Application.* Westport. 149–170.

Schiller, B. (2007a): Pädagogische Nothilfe. Hilfe für traumatisierte Kinder im Libanon. In *Erziehungskunst. Zeitschrift zur Pädagogik Rudolf Steiners.* Stuttgart. 71. Jg., 2/Februar 2007. 171–174.

---. (2007b): Von Berlin nach Baalbek. Pädagogische Nothilfe. In *Erziehungskunst. Monatszeitschrift zur Pädagogik Rudolf Steiners.* Stuttgart. 71. Jg., 6/Juni 2007. 681–683.

Schiller, F. (o. J.): Das verschleierte Bild zu Sais. In Netolitzky, R.: *Friedrich Schiller. Gesammelte Werke in fünf Bänden. Dritter Band: Dramatische Dichtungen III. Gedichte.* Gütersloh. 452–455.

---. (o. J.): Über die ästhetische Erziehung des Menschen. In Netolitzky, R.: *Friedrich Schiller. Gesammelte Werke in fünf Bänden. Fünfter Band: Schriften zur Kunst und Philosophie.* Gütersloh. 287–390.

Schiller, H. (1992): Die Kindheit im Schicksal der Gegenwart–Die erzieherisch-therapeutische Aufgabe von Rhythmus. In Kranich, E. M.; Patzlaff, R.; Schiller, H.; Schuchhardt, M. (1992): *Die Bedeutung des Rhythmus in der Erziehung. Beiträge zur Pädagogik Rudolf Steiners.* 2. 11–42.

———. (2011): *Die Suche nach dem Unverlorenen. Von der Gegenwart des Christus in der Wirklichkeit.* Stuttgart.

Schiller, P. E. (1979): *Der anthroposophische Schulungsweg. Ein Überblick.* Dornach.

Schneider, F. (2010a): *Schläft ein Wort in allen Dingen. Bewegung und Sprache. Vokale.* Stuttgart.

———. (2010b): *Schläft ein Wort in allen Dingen. Bewegung und Sprache. Konsonanten.* Stuttgart.

Schneider, J. (2000): *Der Doppelgänger. Die Schattenseite unserer selbst.* Dornach.

Schopka, G. (2010): Schwertfechten in der Praxis. In Birnthaler, M. (Hrsg.) (2010): *Praxisbuch Erlebnispädagogik.* Stuttgart. 162–171.

Schuberth, E. (1998): Rechenschwächen. Diagnosen, Erscheinungsformen, Therapie. In Glöckler, M. (1998b3): *Das Schulkind–Gemeinsame Aufgaben von Arzt und Lehrer. Konstitutionsfragen, Unterrichtsschwierigkeiten, therapeutische Lehrplanprinzipien.* Persephone 2. Dornach. 235–264.

Schuster, M. (1994): *Kinderzeichnungen. Wie sie entstehen, was sie bedeuten.* Berlin/Heidelberg.

———. (20003): *Psychologie der Kinderzeichnung.* Göttingen.

Seewald, J. (2000): Durch Bewegung zur Identität? In *motorik.* 23 (3). 94–101.

Selg, P. (2005): *Eine grandiose Metamorphose. Zur geisteswissenschaftlichen Anthropologie und Pädagogik des Jugendalters.* Dornach (*A Grand Metamorphosis: Contributions to the Spiritual-Scientific Anthropology and Education of Adolescents.* Great Barrington, MA: SteinerBooks, 2009).

———. (2006): *Vom Logos menschlicher Physis. Die Entfaltung einer anthroposophischen Humanphysiologie im Werk Rudolf Steiners.* Zwei Bände. Dornach.

———. (2010): *Ungeborenheit.* Arlesheim (*Unbornness: Human Pre-existence and the Journey toward Birth.* Great Barrington, MA: SteinerBooks, 2010).

———. (2011): *«Ich bin anders als Du» Vom Selbst- und Welterleben des Kindes in der Mitte der Kindheit.* Arlesheim (*I Am Different From You: How Children Experience Themselves and the World in the Middle of Childhood.* Great Barrington, MA: SteinerBooks, 2011).

Selg, P.; Heusser, P. (2011b): *Das Leib-Seele-Problem. Zur Entwicklung eines geistgemässen Menschenbildes in der Medizin des 20. Jahrhunderts.* Arlesheim.

Senckel, B. (2007): «Wunden, die die Zeit nicht heilt»–Trauma und geistige Behinderung. In *Traumapädagogik. Heilpädagogische Zugänge zu*

Bibliography

Menschen mit Traumata. Fachakademie für Heilpädagogik. Regensburg. 49–58.

Senn, B. (2007): Das Hüttenbauen in der psychomotorischen Therapie. In Buchmann, T. (Hrsg.) (2007): *Psychomotorik-Therapie und individuelle Entwicklung. Bewegung bewegt das Denken und Fühlen.* Luzern. 63–65.

Servan-Schreiber, D. (2006): *Die neue Medizin der Emotionen. Stress, Angst, Depression: Gesund werden ohne Medikamente.* München.

Siegloch, M.; Maier-Smits, L. (1993): *Die erste Eurythmistin. Die Anfänge der Eurythmie.* Dornach.

Smit, J. (1989): *Der werdende Mensch. Zur meditativen Vertiefung des Erziehens.* Stuttgart.

Soesman, A. (2000): *Die zwölf Sinne. Tore der Seele.* Stuttgart.

Der Spiegel (2011a): Starkes Blau. Der französische Apnoe-Taucher Guillaume Néry über die Jagd nach neuen Tiefrekorden und die Kunst, acht Minuten die Luft anzuhalten. Nr. 32 vom 08.08.2011. 134–136.

Der Spiegel (2011b): Die Ware Hunger. Nr. 35 vom 29.08.2011. 75–80.

Spitzer, M. (2003): *Lernen. Gehirnforschung und die Schule des Lebens.* Heidelberg/Berlin.

Staley, B. (1995): *Pubertät. Überleben zwischen Anpassung und Freiheit.* Stuttgart (*Between Form and Freedom: Being a Teenager.* Stroud, UK: Hawthorn Press, 2009).

Steele, W.; Raider, M. (2001): *Structured Sensory Intervention for Traumatized Children, Adolescents and Parents.* Vol. 1, Mellen Studies in Social Work Series. Lewiston, NY: Edwin Mellen Press.

Steiner, R. (1973/CW 4): *Die Philosophie der Freiheit.* Dornach (*Intuitive Thinking as a Spiritual Path: A Philosophy of Freedom.* Hudson, NY: Anthroposophic Press, 1994).

———. (1987/CW 9): *Theosophie.* Dornach (*Theosophy: An Introduction to the Spiritual Processes in Human Life and in the Cosmos.* Hudson, NY: Anthroposophic Press, 1994).

———. (1994/CW 10). *How to Know Higher Worlds: A Modern Path of Initiation* (tr. C. Bamford). Hudson, NY: Anthroposophic Press. CW 10.

———. (1997/CW 13). *An Outline of Esoteric Science* (tr. C. Creeger). Hudson, NY: Anthroposophic Press.

———. (1976/CW 21): *Von Seelenrätseln.* Dornach (*Riddles of the Soul.* Spring Valley, NY: Mercury Press, 1996).

———. (1987/CW 34): Die Erziehung des Kindes vom Gesichtspunkt der Geisteswissenschaft. In Steiner, R. (1987², CW 34): *Luzifer-Gnosis 1903–1908. Grundlegende Aufsätze zur Anthroposophie und Berichte aus der Zeitschrift ‹Luzifer› und ‹Luzifer-Gnosis›.* Dornach. 309–344.

———. (1976/CW 93a): *Grundelemente der Esoterik.* Dornach.

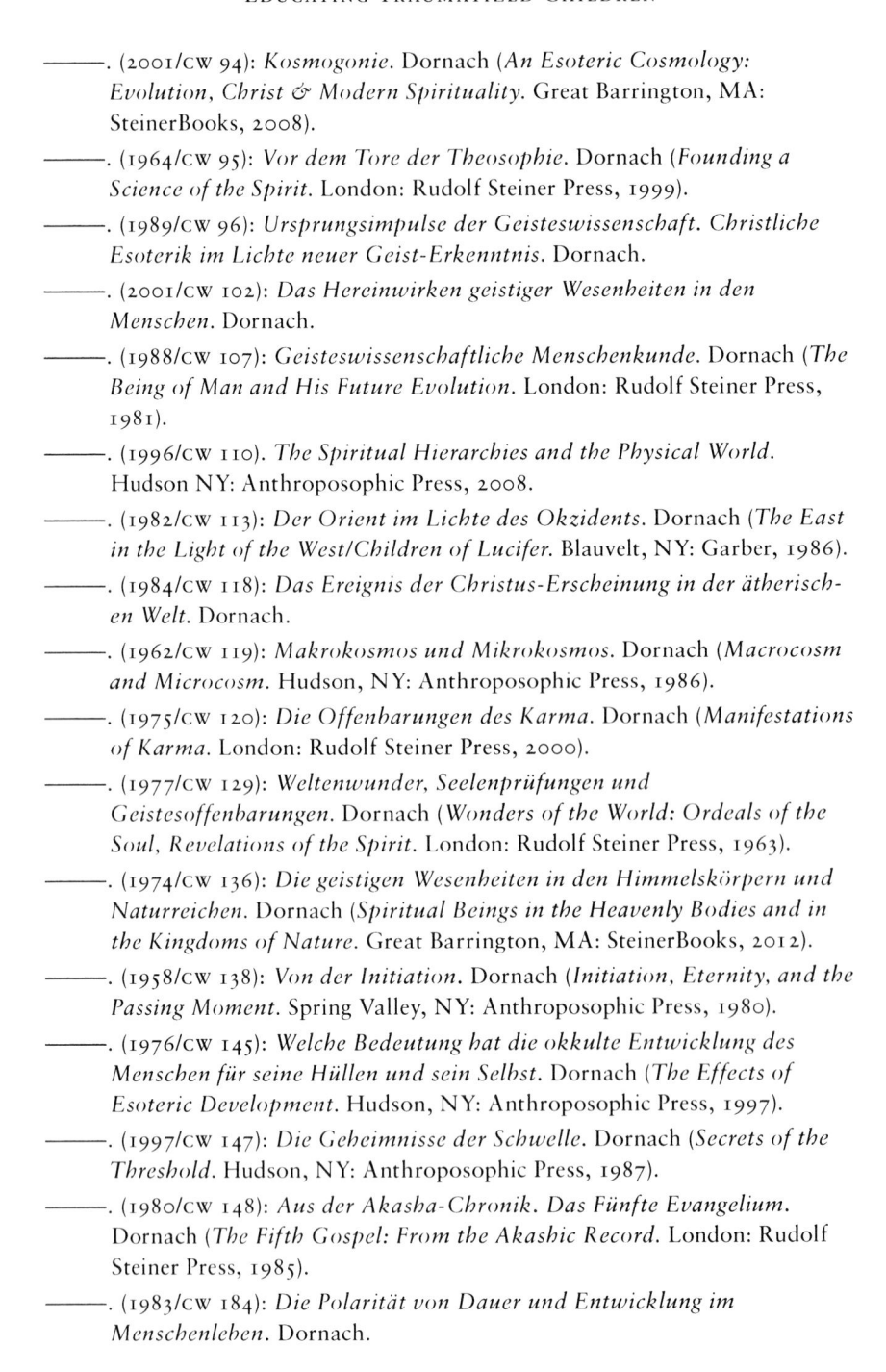

———. (2001/CW 94): *Kosmogonie*. Dornach (*An Esoteric Cosmology: Evolution, Christ & Modern Spirituality*. Great Barrington, MA: SteinerBooks, 2008).

———. (1964/CW 95): *Vor dem Tore der Theosophie*. Dornach (*Founding a Science of the Spirit*. London: Rudolf Steiner Press, 1999).

———. (1989/CW 96): *Ursprungsimpulse der Geisteswissenschaft. Christliche Esoterik im Lichte neuer Geist-Erkenntnis*. Dornach.

———. (2001/CW 102): *Das Hereinwirken geistiger Wesenheiten in den Menschen*. Dornach.

———. (1988/CW 107): *Geisteswissenschaftliche Menschenkunde*. Dornach (*The Being of Man and His Future Evolution*. London: Rudolf Steiner Press, 1981).

———. (1996/CW 110). *The Spiritual Hierarchies and the Physical World*. Hudson NY: Anthroposophic Press, 2008.

———. (1982/CW 113): *Der Orient im Lichte des Okzidents*. Dornach (*The East in the Light of the West/Children of Lucifer*. Blauvelt, NY: Garber, 1986).

———. (1984/CW 118): *Das Ereignis der Christus-Erscheinung in der ätherischen Welt*. Dornach.

———. (1962/CW 119): *Makrokosmos und Mikrokosmos*. Dornach (*Macrocosm and Microcosm*. Hudson, NY: Anthroposophic Press, 1986).

———. (1975/CW 120): *Die Offenbarungen des Karma*. Dornach (*Manifestations of Karma*. London: Rudolf Steiner Press, 2000).

———. (1977/CW 129): *Weltenwunder, Seelenprüfungen und Geistesoffenbarungen*. Dornach (*Wonders of the World: Ordeals of the Soul, Revelations of the Spirit*. London: Rudolf Steiner Press, 1963).

———. (1974/CW 136): *Die geistigen Wesenheiten in den Himmelskörpern und Naturreichen*. Dornach (*Spiritual Beings in the Heavenly Bodies and in the Kingdoms of Nature*. Great Barrington, MA: SteinerBooks, 2012).

———. (1958/CW 138): *Von der Initiation*. Dornach (*Initiation, Eternity, and the Passing Moment*. Spring Valley, NY: Anthroposophic Press, 1980).

———. (1976/CW 145): *Welche Bedeutung hat die okkulte Entwicklung des Menschen für seine Hüllen und sein Selbst*. Dornach (*The Effects of Esoteric Development*. Hudson, NY: Anthroposophic Press, 1997).

———. (1997/CW 147): *Die Geheimnisse der Schwelle*. Dornach (*Secrets of the Threshold*. Hudson, NY: Anthroposophic Press, 1987).

———. (1980/CW 148): *Aus der Akasha-Chronik. Das Fünfte Evangelium*. Dornach (*The Fifth Gospel: From the Akashic Record*. London: Rudolf Steiner Press, 1985).

———. (1983/CW 184): *Die Polarität von Dauer und Entwicklung im Menschenleben*. Dornach.

Bibliography

———. (1980/CW 190): *Vergangenheits- und Zukunftsimpulse im sozialen Geschehen. Die Hintergründe der sozialen Frage.* Bd. 2. Dornach.

———. (1964/CW 192): *Geisteswissenschaftliche Behandlung sozialer und pädagogischer Fragen.* Dornach.

———. (1978/CW 212): *Menschliches Seelenleben im Zusammenhange mit Welt- und Erdenentwicklung.* Dornach.

———. (1999/CW 229): *Das Miterleben des Jahreslaufs in vier kosmischen Imaginationen.* Dornach.

———. (1978/CW 230): *Der Mensch als Zusammenklang des schaffenden, bildenden und gestaltenden Weltenwortes.* Dornach (*Harmony of the Creative Word: The Human Being & the Elemental, Animal, Plant, and Mineral Kingdoms.* London: Rudolf Steiner Press, 2001).

———. (1973/CW 236): *Esoterische Betrachtungen karmischer Zusammenhänge.* Bd. 2. Dornach (*Karmic Relationships: Esoteric Studies*, vol. 2. London: Rudolf Steiner Press, 1997).

———. (1982/CW 276): *Das Künstlerische in seiner Weltmission.* Dornach.

———. (1968/CW 279): *Eurythmie als sichtbare Sprache.* Dornach (*Eurythmy As Visible Speech.* London: Rudolf Steiner Press, 1984).

———. (1982/CW 286): *Wege zu einem neuen Baustil.* Dornach (*Architecture as a Synthesis of the Arts.* London: Rudolf Steiner Press, 1999).

———. (1992/CW 293): *Allgemeine Menschenkunde als Grundlage der Pädagogik.* Dornach (*The Foundations of Human Experience.* Hudson, NY: Anthroposophic Press, 1996).

———. (1974/CW 294): *Erziehungskunst. MethodischDidaktisches.* Dornach (*Practical Advice to Teachers.* Hudson, NY: Anthroposophic Press, 2000).

———. (1998/CW 297a): *Erziehung zum Leben. Selbsterziehung und pädagogische Praxis.* Dornach.

———. (1971/CW 302): *Menschenerkenntnis und Unterrichtsgestaltung.* Dornach (*Education for Adolescents.* Hudson, NY: Anthroposophic Press, 1996).

———. (1979/CW 304): *Erziehungs- und Unterrichtsmethoden auf anthroposophischer Grundlage.* Dornach (*Waldorf Education and Anthroposophy 1.* Hudson, NY: Anthroposophic Press, 1995).

———. (1991/CW 305): *Die geistig-seelischen Grundkräfte der Erziehungskunst.* Dornach (*The Spiritual Ground of Education.* Hudson, NY: Anthroposophic Press, 2004).

———. (1995/CW 317): *Heilpädagogischer Kurs.* Dornach (*Education for Special Needs: The Curative Education Course.* London: Rudolf Steiner Press, 1998).

Steiner, R.; Steiner-von-Sievers, M. (1981/CW 282): *Sprachgestaltung und dramatische Kunst*. Dornach (*Speech and Drama*. Great Barrington, MA: SteinerBooks, 2007).

Stellamans-Wellens, H. (2002): *Narben auf der Seele. Traumatisierte Kinder und ihre Eltern*. Stuttgart.

Stevenson, R. (1981): *Der seltsame Fall von Dr. Jekyll und Mr. Hyde*. (Ohne Ortsangabe).

Straube, M.; Hasselberg, R. (1994): *Schwellenerlebnisse–Grenzerfahrungen. Krisensituationen in der Biographie*. Stuttgart.

Strauss, M. (1977): *Von der Zeichensprache des kleinen Kindes. Spuren der Menschwerdung. Menschenkunde und Erziehung 34*. Stuttgart.

Streeck-Fischer, A. (1999): *Adoleszenz und Trauma*. Göttingen.

Tedeschi, R. G.; Calhoun, L. G. (1996): The posttraumatic growth inventory: measuring the positive legacy of trauma. In *Journal of Traumatic Stress*. 9 (3), 1996. 455ff.

Tedeschi, R. G.; Park, C. L.; Calhoun, L. G. (1998): *Postraumatic growth: positive changes in the aftermath of crisis*. New York.

Teegen, F. (2003): *Posttraumatische Belastungsstörung bei gefährdeten Berufsgruppen. Prävalenz–Prävention–Behandlung*. Bern.

Terr, L. C. (1995): Childhood traumas: An outline and an overview. In Everly, G.; Lating J. (Hrsg.) (1995): *Psychotraumatology: Key Papers and Core Concepts in Post-Traumatic Stress*. New York: Plenum Press, 301–319.

Thomas, A.; Thomas, P. (2006): *Das grosse Ferien- und Freizeitbuch*. Stuttgart.

Treichler, M. (1993a): *Sprechstunde Psychotherapie. Krisen-Krankheiten an Leib und Seele. Wege zur Bewältigung*. Stuttgart.

Treichler, R. (1984): *Was ist anthroposophische Psychiatrie?* Dornach.

———. (1993b): Grundzüge einer geisteswissenschaftlich orientierten Psychiatrie. In Husemann, W. (1993): *Das Bild des Menschen als Grundlage der Heilkunst*. Bd. 3. Stuttgart.

———. (1995): Angst. In *Flensburger Hefte*. Nr. 48/1995. 30–81.

Ulich, D. (1987): *Krise und Entwicklung. Zur Psychologie der seelischen Gesundheit*. München.

Vandercruysse, R. (1999): *Die therapeutische Dimension des Denkens. Anthroposophische Aspekte zur Psychoanalyse*. Stuttgart.

van der Kolk, B. A. (1999): Zur Psychologie und Psychobiologie von Kindheitstraumata (Developmental Trauma). In Streeck-Fischer, A. (1999): *Adoleszenz und Trauma*. Göttingen.

van der Stel, A. (2011): Somatische Entwicklungsproblematik. In Niemeijer, M. et al. (2011): *Entwicklungsstörungen bei Kindern undJugendlichen. Medizinisch-pädagogische Begleitung und Behandlung*. Stuttgart. 173–188.

Bibliography

van Lommel, P. (2009): *Endloses Bewusstsein. Neue medizinische Fakten zur Nahtoderfahrung.* Düsseldorf.

Vogel, N. F. (Hrsg.) (2007): *Heileurythmie für Kinder. Mit Übungen aus dem Lebenswerk von Anne-Maidlin Vogel.* Dornach.

Wais, M. (1993): *Biografiearbeit–Lebensberatung.* Stuttgart.

Wais, M.; Schellenberg, U. (1998): *Trennung und Abschied. Der Mensch auf dem Wege.* Stuttgart/Berlin.

Walter-Baumgartner, J. (2011): Rhythmisch-musikalische Sprech-, Sing- und Bewegungsspiele. In Compani, M.-L.; Lang, P. (2011): *Waldorfkindergarten heute. Eine Einführung.* Stuttgart. 157–178.

Watkins, H. H., and J. Watkins. (2003): *Ego-States. Theorie und Therapie: Ein Handbuch.* Heidelberg.

Weihrauch, W. (1994): Der Hüter der Schwelle. In *Hüter der Schwelle. Der Mensch am Abgrund. Flensburger Hefte.* 45, 6/1994. 91–153.

Weiss, W. (2006): *Philipp sucht sein Ich. Zum pädagogischen Umgang mit Traumata in der Entwicklungshilfe.* Weinheim/München.

Welter-Enderlin, R.; Hildenbrand, B. (Hrsg.) (2008): *Resilienz–Gedeihen trotz widriger Umstände.* Heidelberg.

Wilde, O. (1985): *Das Bildnis des Dorian Gray.* München (*The Picture of Dorian Gray*).

Windeck, I. (1984): *Förderung Verhaltensgestörter und Lernbehinderter in Waldorf-Sonderschuleinrichtungen.* Bonn/Bad Godesberg.

Wolf, K. (1998): Sozialpädagogische Betreuung oder Behandlung? Kinder zwischen Heimerziehung und Psychiatrie. In Köttgen, C. (Hrsg.): *Wenn alle Stricke reissen: Kinder und Jugendliche zwischen Erziehung, Therapie und Strafe.* Bonn. 46ff.

Wothe, K. (2001): Belastungsfaktoren im Einsatz. In Puzicha et al. (Hrsg.): *Psychologie für Einsatz und Notfall.* Bonn. 65–71.

Zaleski, C. (1993): *Nah-Todeserlebnisse und Jenseitsvisionen vom Mittelalter bis zur Gegenwart.* Frankfurt/Leipzig.

Zimmermann, H. (1997): *Von den Auftriebskräften in der Erziehung.* Dornach.

Zinke, J. (2003): *Lautformen sichtbar gemacht. Die Sprache als plastische Gestaltung der Luft.* Hg. von R. Patzlaff. Stuttgart.

Zumpfe, H. (1999): Aus dem Tagebuch der kleinen Kinder. Kinderzeichnungen als Symptome der Entwicklung. In *Erziehungskunst. Monatsschrift zur Pädagogik Rudolf Steiners.* 9, September 1999. 967–979.

About the Author

Bernd Ruf was born in Karlsruhe, Germany, in 1954. He trained as a secondary school teacher at Mannheim University, specializing in German and history before gaining additional qualifications as a special needs teacher (Reutlingen) and as a Waldorf teacher (Stuttgart). Bernd Ruf cofounded the Waldorf school in Karlsruhe, where he also taught for twenty years, and the Parzival Kompetenzzentrum für Bildung, Förderung und Beratung, a special needs education center that is based on the principles of Waldorf education. Ruf has been director at Parzival since 2003. From 1993 to 2007 he was a board member of the Bund der Freien Waldorfschulen (Federal Association of Waldorf Schools) in Germany. Since 1993 he has been a member of the International Forum of Waldorf Schools and, since 1987, he has been Managing Director of the aid organization Friends of Waldorf Education where he is in charge of International Volunteer Services. He has been heading emergency education crisis interventions in war and disaster zones since 2006. These interventions have led him to Lebanon, China, the Gaza Strip, Indonesia, Haiti, Kyrgyzstan, Japan, and Kenya. He is head of the Emergency Education Service at the Karlsruhe Parzival Center and has been on the Advisory Council to the Federal Ministry for Economic Cooperation and Development since 2007. Bernd Ruf lectures and offers seminars in many countries.

Ita Wegman Institute
for Basic Research into Anthroposophy

Pfeffinger Weg 1 a CH 4144 Arlesheim, Switzerland
www.wegmaninstitute.ch
e-mail: sekretariat@wegmaninstitute.ch

The Ita Wegman Institute for Basic Research into Anthroposophy is a non-profit research and teaching organization. It undertakes basic research into the lifework of Dr. Rudolf Steiner (1861–1925) and the application of Anthroposophy in specific areas of life, especially medicine, education, and curative education. Work carried out by the Institute is supported by a number of foundations and organizations and an international group of friends and supporters. The Director of the Institute is Prof. Dr. Peter Selg.